DATE DUE			
FEB 29 '96			
MAR 22 '02			

BAD BOY

OJIBWAY ORATORY

GREAT MOMENTS IN THE RECORDED SPEECH OF THE CHIPPEWA, 1695-1889

TAKE ALL THE WORDS

AND GATHER THEM TOGETHER

WITH YOUR FINGERS

AND SAVE THEM

IN YOUR BREAST.

Majigabo (1858)

COMPILED AND ILLUSTRATED BY

Mark Diedrich

coyote books

ROCHESTER, MINNESOTA

Dedicated to the memory of two who cared:

Peter W. Cadwell (1949-1988)

and

Alyce M. Bergey (1934-1989)

I have lost my memory. The Ojibbeways have all lost their memory. The Americans have made them weak....Our nation is fallen; and this came quite suddenly, since the Kitchimokomans, or 'Long-knives,' entered our country....the Long-knives brought us even more whiskey-water than the Englishman, and these killed more men and animals for us, and the times always became worse, worse. The presents and the salt pork grew ever worse, and the hunting-grounds have failed: besides, more and more land was taken from us....since the copper mines have been discovered, and the great steamers have appeared on the lake [Superior] , and since the canal has been dug, which brings their ships easily from Huron Lake into our waters, and that all the men have come to seek copper, and look at our lake, it has been all over with the Ojibbeways. Their strength is broken, and they have lost their memory. Their tribes have melted away, their chiefs have no voice in council. Their wise men and priests have no longer good dreams, and the old squaws forget their good stories and fables.

Aurora (an Ojibway woman) to
Johann G. Kohl, 1855

Library of Congress Catalog Number: 89-081116
ISBN 0-9616901-4-3
Printed in the United States of America.

Cover illustration: Flat Mouth II, by Mark Diedrich, 1989
Frontispiece: Bad Boy, by Mark Diedrich, 1989

Contents

* * * * *

ILLUSTRATIONS BY MARK DIEDRICH:

WHITE FISHER

Introduction

"I have great influence with the upper Indians, and when I put words in their hearts they are not soon forgotten or lightly regarded." --Flat Mouth, 1850

THIS VOLUME IS DEVOTED to the speeches (and the stories behind them) of the Ojibway, or Chippewa, people, culled from almost two centuries of their history. It is envisioned as a companion volume to the previously published **Dakota Oratory**. The speeches were made by some forty-four individuals from about twenty different locations--from Sault Ste. Marie to Turtle Mountain. Featured are such prominent orators as Shingaba-ossin, Broken Tooth, Flat Mouth, the elder and younger Hole-in-the-Days, White Cloud, and many others for the most part unknown to history.

According to their traditional history, the Ojibways once lived near the Gulf of the St. Lawrence River, from whence they began to migrate westward to Sault Ste. Marie. It was here that they were discovered by the French, who referred to them logically as the "Saulters." By the late 1600s portions of the tribe migrated westward along the southern shores of Lake Superior, establishing a major village on Madeline Island in Chequamegon Bay. From this vantage point, Ojibway hunting bands, usually made up of a few extended families, began to occupy points in northern Wisconsin such as Lac du Flambeau, Lac Court Orielles, and the St. Croix River. During the 1700s other Ojibways attained to dominance of northern Minnesota as well, replacing the Sioux tribes which had begun to migrate to the south and west (The two tribes became hereditary enemies during this period, and warfare between the various bands continued off and on for over a century.) Then,with permanent villages located at Fond du Lac, Sandy Lake, Leech Lake, and Red Lake, other Ojibways pressed west, out of the forests and onto the plains, with campgrounds at Pembina and Turtle Mountain. (Other Ojibways occupied the region north of Lake Superior and westward as far as Saskatchewan--these being called the Plains Chippewa, or Saulteaux, but they are not represented in this book, as their history is somewhat alien to the American Ojibways.)

ORATORICAL ABILITY was a gift well-respected among the Ojibways as it was the principle means of formulating public opinion and concensus of action: orators thus became prominent in the leadership of their people. When a hereditary chief was also an able orator, there was the possibility that his influence might extend beyond the traditional bounds of his family, kin, and band unit and affect the Ojibways regionally. In other words, an orator could transcend the limitations of the patriarchal, yet democratic, Ojibway government, and the fact that they had no supreme, or head, chief office. William Keating (with the Long expedition of 1823) commented that the Ojibways "have no national councils" due to their "dispersed condition." And the great Flat Mouth admitted the governmental limitation of his people in 1837, saying "I am not the chief of the whole nation; but only of my people, or band." Furthermore, as Chingouabe stated in 1695 the hereditary chiefs did not even have authority to command obedience to their wishes. Rather, councils had to be held allowing the men to speak out freely on the issues facing them. The chiefs and headmen, or elders, refined the various viewpoints and came to an eventual decision on what position to take, particularly in regard to dealings with the whites. When a meeting was to be held with important government officials, a speaker was appointed by the chiefs and headmen to convey their feelings. Again, if a chief was an orator, he was doubly influential. Flat Mouth was such an individual--even in old age a white observer wrote that the chief "was looked upon as the finest orator among all the Indians"; that when he "warmed with his subject he exerted a powerful influence over his auditors." Hole-in-the-Day, the Elder, was another--Julius Clark stated that when this chief spoke he "looked the personification of ELOQUENCE itself." But although both of these men were present for the treaty council of 1837, it was the orator, Majigabo, who became the principal speaker for the Ojibway bands gathered from all over Wisconsin and Minnesota. He was not a chief, but spoke "in the name of the chiefs." He boasted that he "was descended from those who in former days were the greatest orators" of his nation. Similarly, an Ojibway speaker stated at a council at Fond du Lac in 1826: "It is not I alone who speak. The chiefs and old men of my band put words in my mouth." It is evident that the orators helped their people overcome the confusion resulting from having no head chief to speak or represent the many far-flung bands, particularly when large councils were held to discuss important treaty-related matters. They helped bring the young men to some concensus, represented the positions of the various chiefs, and relayed all of the concerns coherently and comprehensively to the white officials. Still, the Ojibways were at a tremendous disadvantage when dealing with the government and poor treaties often resulted despite all of their efforts. Hole-in-the-Sky alluded to the failure of the Ojibway "political system" in 1855 when he said that the suffering of his tribe was the result of the "folly" of their chiefs, who too often failed to consult adequately with the young men, being more influenced by "other parties" (no doubt referring to the powerful trading companies, as well as the mixed-blood factions, the missionaries, agents, etc..) At any rate, orators were highly respected individuals and certainly played an instrumental role in the history of their people.

At a typical council, the Ojibways would sit on the ground, with the chiefs and orators in front, usually smoking their pipes and wearing their finest costumes. There was silence generally and profound decorum. When the time came to respond to the whites, those who had been selected beforehand would rise one by one to speak (first shaking hands with all of the prominent whites present.) They spoke in their own individual styles, ranging from graceful in manner and brief in words, to wild gesticulatory movements and great length of speech. Flat Mouth II was one of the former: a reporter wrote in 1866, "His words are few but to the point. In manner he is graceful, and in utterance fluent and forcible." Sits Ahead was one of the latter: in 1855 his oratory was described as "rapid and vehement--his gestures quick and flashy; his whole action and look, when excited in speech, so wild that they similate the maniac."

Most of the speeches herein were of necessity recorded by white people, particularly government agents like Lawrence Taliaferro and Henry Schoolcraft, treaty recorders, newspaper reporters, missionaries, and travelers. Hence, almost all of the speeches were addressed to the whites and usually were about Indian-white relations. The interpreters were generally men of mixed blood (with Ojibway-white ancestry), like William Warren, Paul Beaulieu, and Peter Roy; they were undoubtedly fluent in Ojibway but not necessarily educated in English. What was lost in the translation and recording of these speeches cannot now be determined or rectified. However, despite the aforementioned limitations, the body of speeches in this collection are an invaluable expression of how the Ojibways felt, reacted, and responded at particular points in time, demonstrating as no history book can their character, beliefs, and attitudes on the great issues of their lives.

Mark Diedrich

SWEET

CHAPTER ONE

THE FRENCH AND BRITISH PERIOD, 1695-1816

"I do not wish to meddle in their quarrels."

"...I cannot answer, except for myself."

CHINGOUABE July 18, 1695

CHINGOUABE was a chief of the Ojibways who inhabited Madeline Island, in Chequamegon Bay of southwestern Lake Superior. In 1695 he accompanied the French trader Le Sueur, and the Dakota chief Tiyoskate, to Montreal. In a council with governor-general Frontenac, Chingouabe said that the Ojibways were allies of the Sioux, and that the two tribes wanted to make war on two enemy tribes--the Fox and Mascouten. Frontenac, however, advised the chief not to meddle in the Sioux wars. Chingouabe then explained that, although he might personally wish to take this advice, he had no real authority to make his people comply with it--that there were distinct limitations to his control over his tribe as opposed to the French system of government. Le Sueur, who spoke both the Ojibway and Dakota languages, was the probable interpreter on this occasion.

> **Father! it is not the same with us, as with you. When you command, all the French obey you and go to war. But I shall not be heeded and obeyed by my nation in like manner. Therefore I cannot answer, except for myself and those immediately allied or related to me. Nevertheless I shall communicate your pleasure to all the Sauteurs [People of Sault Ste. Marie--or Ojibway], and in order that you may be satisfied of what I say, I will invite the French [men] who are in my village to be witnesses of what I shall tell my people in your behalf.**

The Ojibways of Lake Superior remained on fairly good terms with the Sioux for several decades afterwards. But later they became middlemen in the French trade to the Crees, who were bitter enemies of the Dakota. Warfare then broke out between the former allies which continued off and on for a century and a half. The date of Chingouabe's death is not known. By the mid-1700s Big Feet was a leading chief of the Madeline Island Ojibway, and he was the father of the renowned war chief and leader, White Fisher (Waubojeeg).

Source: Edward D. Neill, "History of the Ojibways," 420-22, in William W. Warren, *History of the Ojibway* (Minneapolis: Ross and Haines, Inc., 1974).

"...you have conquered the French, you have not yet conquered us!"

MINNEHWEHNA Spring 1761

THE EASTERN PORTION of the Ojibway tribe lived at the head of Lake Michigan, not far from the old French fort and trading post at Michilimackinac. After the French and Indian war, British troops occupied the fort. In the spring of 1761 an Ojibway war chief named Minnehwehna visited the post and spoke with trader Alexander Henry. The trader described the chief as a person of remarkable appearance, with a commanding stature, and singularly fine countenance. The chief spoke of his tribe's attachment to the French:

> **Englishman! You know that the French king is our father. He promised to be such; and we in return promised to be his children. This promise we have kept.**
>
> **Englishman! It is you that have made war with this our father....We are informed that our father, the king of France, is old and infirm; and that being fatigued with making war upon your nation, he is fallen asleep. During his sleep you have taken advantage of him and possessed yourselves of Canada. But his nap is almost at an end. I think I hear him already stirring and inquiring for his children, the Indians: and when he does awake, what must become of you? He will destroy you utterly.**
>
> **Englishman! Although you have conquered the French, you have not yet conquered us! We are not your slaves. These lakes and these woods and mountains were left to us by our ancestors. They are our inheritance, and we will part with them to none. Your nation supposes that we, like the white people, cannot live without bread and pork and beef. But you ought to know that he--the Great Spirit and Master of Life--has provided food for us in these broad lakes and upon these mountains.**
>
> **Englishman! Our father, the king of France, employed our young men to make war on your nation. In this warfare many of them have been killed, and it is our custom to retaliate until such time as the spirits of the slain are satisfied in either of two ways. The first is by spilling the blood of the nation by whom they fell; and the other, by covering the bodies of the dead, and thus allaying the resentment of their relatives. This is done by making presents.**
>
> **Englishman! Your king has never sent us any presents, nor entered into any treaty with us, wherefore, he and we are still at war; and until he does these things, we must consider that we have no other father or friend among the white men than the king of France....**

Due to the failure of the British leaders to woo the tribes over to the king of Britain by giving presents, a number of Great Lakes tribes rose up against the English in the Pontiac War. Minnehwehna was a leader of the Ojibway in the attack and capture of Fort Michilimackinac on June 4, 1763.

Source: Warren, *History of the Ojibway*, 196-200. Other Ojibway participants in the Pontiac War (particularly the siege of Fort Detroit) were Wasson and 250 Saginaw Bay warriors, and Sekahos with 170 warriors of the Mississaugi-Chippewas from the Thames River. See, Howard H. Peckham, *Pontiac and the Indian Uprising* (Chicago: Phoenix Books, 1961), 182.

"I fought hand to hand at the head of my band...."

WHITE FISHER 1783

WHITE FISHER was one of the greatest heroes of the Ojibway. Born about 1747, his father was Big Feet (Mamongazida), who was half-brother to the great Dakota chief, Wabasha I. Unlike his father, who fought for the French under Montcalm at Quebec in 1759, White Fisher refused to be involved in wars between the European powers. Instead, he devoted himself to warfare against tribal enemies, particularly the Dakota and Fox (According to Schoolcraft, White Fisher thus had "a more patriotic object for his achievement.") The young war chief led a total of seven expeditions against his enemies and was wounded three times in battle. His most famous fight was against the Dakota and Fox at St. Croix Falls after the close of the American Revolutionary War in 1783. Although the Ojibways suffered severe losses, including the brother of White Fisher, the victory drove the Fox tribe forever from north-central Wisconsin. White Fisher composed a war song after the battle which was preserved in stanzas by the chief's later son-in-law, John Johnston of Sault Ste. Marie:

On that day when our heroes lay low--lay low,
On that day when our heroes lay low,
I fought by their side, and thought ere I died,
Just vengeance to take on the foe,
Just vengeance to take on the foe.

On that day when our chieftains lay dead--lay dead,
On that day when our chieftains lay dead,
I fought hand to hand, at the head of my band,
And here on my breast have I bled,
And here on my breast have I bled.

Our chiefs shall return no more--no more,
Our chiefs shall return no more,
Nor their brothers of war, who can show scar for scar,
Like women their fate shall deplore,
Like women their fate shall deplore.

My friends when my spirit is fled--is fled,
My friends when my spirit is fled,
Put me not bound in the dark and cold ground,
Where light shall not longer be shed--be shed,
Where day light no more shall be shed.

The chief died ten years after the battle, in 1793, at his native village of La Pointe, on Madeline Island. He was forty-five years old. Sometime before, he agreed to allow his daughter to marry a white man, John Johnston, but not before making the following quip: "White man, I have noticed your behavior: it has been correct, but white man, your color is deceitful." This marriage produced a daughter who became the wife of the noted Ojibway agent and explorer, Henry R. Schoolcraft.

Source: Henry R. Schoolcraft, *The Literary Voyager; or Muzzeniegun*, Philip P. Mason, ed. (East Lansing, Michigan: Michigan State University Press, 1962), 41-42, 50-56.

"The Master of Life has given to all the Indians the land to live on in peace...."

LE COEUR D'OURS November 1788

BY ABOUT THE MID-1700s, Ojibway hunters from La Pointe began to occupy the region about Lac Court Orielle, where a permanent village was eventually established. With the defeat of the Fox in 1783, the Ojibways hunted ever southward, though there was still ever-present danger from attacks by Mdewakanton Dakota bands who hunted in western Wisconsin. In 1788 Le Coeur d'Ours and six of his men visited the trading post of Jean Perrault on the Red Cedar River (near present-day Menomonie). While they were trading their furs, the Dakota band of Petit Corbeau (or Little Crow) arrived. He asked Le Coeur d'Ours to allow the Dakotas to hunt deer on Ojibway lands as "upon it depends the life of our women and children." Le Coeur d'Ours replied:

> **My brothers, we are well pleased to see you here and to be able to say to you in the presence of the French, that you need have no anxiety on our account. Hunt peaceably on our lands here till the month of March, when we beg of you to withdraw, and that your young men come not here and frighten our children at that time. The Master of Life has given to all the Indians the land to live on in peace, but unhappily, we are all foolish.**

The chief's words were all too prophetic. That evening some "illtimed words" were exchanged between the hunters of the two tribes, and the following day the Dakotas ambushed and killed one of the Ojibways. Another Ojibway, who was mortally wounded, was brought back to the trading post. Instead of blaming the Dakotas, he castigated the French traders for sending the Ojibways away shortly after the Sioux had departed. Just before expiring, he added: "You do not trouble yourselves much about the Indians so long as you can get the packs."

Source: Jean B. Perrault, "Narrative of the Travels and Adventures, 1783-1820," *Michigan Pioneer and Historical Collections* 37 (1909-10):547-550.

"...he gave us assurance that all our lands should remain to us...."

EASTERN OJIBWAY CHIEFS 1795 and 1797

WHILE SOME OJIBWAY CHIEFS, like White Fisher, tried to remain aloof from conflicts between the white powers, others took sides. Various Ojibway warriors under Matchikiwis, for example, joined the British campaign against St. Louis in 1780 during the American Revolutionary War. Then, in 1788 the eastern Ojibways were notified that General Arthur St. Clair, the U.S. governor of the Northwest Territory, wished to sign a treaty with them to extinguish Indian title to land which the American government wanted. The Ojibway chief Massass was a signer of the January 1789 treaty at Fort Harmar. But in 1791 some of the Ojibways joined the Miami chief, Little Turtle, in their battle against General St. Clair's soldiers on the upper Wabash River, destroying about half of the 1,300 man force! However, three years later, the confederated Indian tribes were defeated by General Anthony Wayne at the battle of Fallen Timbers. Eleven Ojibway leaders, including young Buffalo, and Massass, attended peace talks held at Fort Greenville in the summer of 1795. Massass complained that the Ojibways had never received compensation for the lands they ceded by the treaty at Fort Harmar:

> **I was surprised when I heard your voice through a good interpreter say that we have received presents and compensation for those lands which were thereby ceded. I tell you now, that we, the three fires, never were informed of it. If our uncles, the Wyandots, and grandfathers, the Delawares, have received such presents, they have kept them to themselves. I always thought that we, the Ottawas, Chippewas, and Potawatomis, were the true owners of those lands, but now I find that new masters have undertaken to dispose of them; so that at this day we do not know to whom they, of right, belong. We have never received any compensation for them.**

General Wayne apparently assured the Ojibways that all of their lands would remain their own, and Massass, Buffalo, Little Thunder, Bad Bird, and others signed the treaty of 1795. Two years later, in September 1797, various Ojibway chiefs visited with one Major May at Detroit. They spoke of their councils with General Wayne and wanted their requests relayed to their "Great and Good Father at the great village of Philadelphia" (referring apparently to John Adams, who had succeeded George Washington as president earlier that year.)

> **We sometimes since met a great war chief of your people at Greenville for the purpose of putting a happy end to the war subsisting between us, which chief we are told is now gone to the great and good Spirit....**
>
> **In our great council with him, he gave us assurance that all our lands should remain to us and remain to our youths and at our disposal; what passed there, we consider as done before the great and good Spirit that punishes people for doing bad things or tellings that are not true.... We returned home contented to our little houses to see our children and aged parents.**

Sources: Virginia I. Armstrong, comp. *I Have Spoken: American History Through the Voices of the Indians* (Chicago: Sage Books, 1971), 38; William H. Guthman, *March to Massacre, A History of the First Seven Years of the United States Army, 1784-1791* (New York: McGraw-Hill Book Co., 1970), 155-58, 237-43; Ojibway Chiefs' Speech to Major May, September 8, 1797, in *Michigan Pioneer and Historical Collections* 8 (1907):506.

"Will not my pipe answer the same purpose?"

SWEET and FLAT MOUTH February 16, 1806

DURING THE WINTER OF 1805-6, American lieutenant Zebulon M. Pike traveled with a number of soldiers up the Mississippi River to Leech Lake to visit the Ojibway bands in the region. He was met by Sweet, the Red Lake chief, and Chief of the Land and Flat Mouth of the Leech Lake bands. Pike asked the chiefs to make peace with the Sioux, and then go with him to meet General James Wilkinson, the new governor of Louisiana Territory; he also wanted to replace their British medals with American ones. Sweet (Le Sucre) replied in such a way as to firmly decline taking the proposed trip:

> **My father, this medal I hold in my hands I received from the English chiefs. I willingly deliver it up to you. Wabasha's calumet, with which I am presented, I receive with all my heart. Be assured that I will use my best endeavors to keep my young men quiet. There is my calumet. I send it to my father, the great war chief. What does it signify that I should go to see him? Will not my pipe answer the same purpose?**

After a few brief remarks by Chief of the Land, Flat Mouth (Gueule Platte), one of the foremost war chiefs of his nation, responded that in the interests of peace he, also, could not go to St. Louis:

> **My father, my heart beat high with joy when I heard that you had arrived, and that all the nations through which you passed had received and made peace among them....You ask me to accompany you to meet our father, the great war chief. This I would willingly do, but certain considerations prevent me. I have sent my calumet to all the Sauteaux who hunt round about, to assemble to form a war party; should I be absent, they, when assembled, might strike those with whom we have made peace, and thus kill our brothers....**
>
> **I present you with the medal of my uncle here present. He received it from the English chiefs as a recompense for his good hunts. As for me, I have no medal here; it is at my tent, and I will cheerfully deliver it up. That medal was given me by the English traders in consideration of something I had done; and I can say that three-fourths of those here present belong to me....**

Flat Mouth went on to say that he would "bury the hatchet" with the Sioux--that "even should the Sioux come and strike me, for the first time I would not take up the hatchet; but should they come and strike me a second time, I would dig up my hatchet and revenge myself."

Source: Eliott Coues, ed. *The Expeditions of Zebulon Montgomery Pike* (Minneapolis: Ross and Haines, Inc., 1965), 1:254-61, 169-72. Pike was able to convince a chief named Buck and Flat Mouth's brother, Beaux, to make the trip to see Wilkinson.

"...I do not wish to meddle in their quarrels...."

FLAT MOUTH circa 1812

UPON THE OUTBREAK of the War of 1812, the British tried to bring their old Indian allies into it against the Americans. They utilized Robert Dickson, a prominent trader on the upper Mississippi, to persuade many Dakotas, Sac and Fox, Winnebago, and Menominees to join the cause. He sent interpreter St. Germain from Fort William to Leech Lake to gain the cooperation of the Pillager Ojibways under Flat Mouth. At a council, St. Germain presented the chief with presents and Dickson's wampum war belts. The chief, however, sent the belts back, with the answer:

> **When I go to war against my enemies, I do not call on the whites to join my warriors. The white people have quarreled among themselves, and I do not wish to meddle in their quarrels, nor do I intend ever, even to be guilty of breaking the windowglass of a white man's dwelling.**

St. Germain then urged the chief to visit Fort William, but Flat Mouth and all of his warriors, except for one, refused to go.

Source: Warren, *History of the Ojibway*, 368-70.

"I cannot strike my own father."

KEESHKEMUN circa Summer 1812

SHORTLY AFTER THE OUTBREAK of war, the British and their Indian allies captured American-held Fort Howard, at Mackinac, on July 17, 1812. British Indian agents continued to enlist support among the tribes of the region. However, many of the western Ojibways refused to join up with the Redcoats, including the Lac du Flambeau chief, Keeshkemun (Sharpened Stone). British agent John Askin asked the chief why he would not aid them. The chief replied, with interpretation by Michel Cadotte Jr., that, although the British had "put out the fire" of his French father, the Americans (the "Long Knife") had put their hearts on his breast--he then displayed a George Washington medal which he kept in a decorated tobacco pouch. Askin demanded the medal of the chief and made threats against him if he did not help the British. Keeshkemun responded:

> **Englishman! I shall not give up this medal of my own will. If you wish to take it from me, you are stronger than I am. But I tell you, it is but a mere bauble. It is only an emblem of the heart which beats in my bosom; to cut out which you must first kill me!**
>
> **Englishman! You say that you will keep me a prisoner in this, your strong house. You are stronger than I am. You can do as you say. But remember the voice of the crane echoes afar off, and when he summons his children together, they number like the pebbles on the Great Lake shore [referring to his Crane family relations among the scattered Ojibway bands]!**
>
> **....You sent for me wishing to set me on to my father, the Long Knife, as a hunter sets his dogs on a deer. I cannot do as you wish. I cannot strike my own father. He, the Long Knife, has not yet told us to fight for him. Had he done so, you, Englishman, would not now be in this strong house. The Long Knife counsels us to remain quiet. In this do we know that he is our own father, and that he has confidence in the strength of his single arm.**

Keeshkemun's statements regarding American Indian policy during the war were correct. That summer, various Indian leaders from tribes on the Mississippi and Missouri rivers (although not including the Ojibway) were brought to Washington City to meet President James Madison. He told them that he did not need them to join his soldiers--that they could remain as witnesses to see how the Americans won their war and protected their Indian friends.

Source: Warren, *History of the Ojibway*, 372-76. Regarding the Indians' trip to Washington in 1812, see Mark Diedrich, *Famous Chiefs of the Eastern Sioux* (Minneapolis: Coyote Books, 1987), 19-20.

"I thought I carried about me the marks which proved my manhood!"

SWEET circa Summer 1812

SWEET was another of the Ojibway chiefs summoned by the British to Mackinac at the outbreak of the War of 1812. Like others, he was urged to join the British cause with his band of Red Lake warriors. When he steadfastly refused, a British commander resorted to insults, saying "I thought you were men, but I see that you are but women, not fit even to wear the breechclout...." Sweet stood up, and placing his hand on the officer's epaulette, said:

> **Wait, you have spoken; now let me speak. You say that we should not wear the breechcloth, but the dress of women. (Pointing to the old English fort taken by the Ojibway in 1763), Englishman! have you already forgotten that we once made you cry like children? yonder! Who was the woman then?**
>
> **Englishman! you have said that we are women. If you doubt our manhood, you have young men here in your strong house. I have also young men. You must come out on some open place, and we will fight. You will better know whether we are fit or not to wear the breechcloth.**
>
> **Englishman! you have said words which the ears of We-esh-coob [Sweet] have never heard, (and throwing down his blanket in great excitement, he pointed to different scars on his naked body, he exclaimed) I thought I carried about me the marks which proved my manhood.**

The officer apologized for his hasty words, and goodwill was restored, but the bitter taunt helped keep many Ojibways out of the war.

Source: Warren, *History of the Ojibways*, 376-77. Sweet (or Weescoup) signed the 1825 treaty at Prairie du Chien, but apparently died before the 1837 treaty with the U.S. government was made. One Ojibway chief who did join in the war was Oshawahnah. He participated in British campaigns against the Americans in the Ohio country in 1813, and was at the battle on the Thames River where Tecumseh, the Shawnee leader was killed. Oshawahnah afterwards surrendered to Gen. Henry Harrison at Detroit. See, Harrison Bird, *War for the West: 1790-1813* (New York: Oxford University Press, 1971), 247, 254.

"...I find you do not seem inclined to let me draw near your breast."

BROKEN TOOTH July 22, 1816

BROKEN TOOTH was another of the western Ojibway chiefs who was reluctant to become involved in the War of 1812. Yet, as late as 1815 certain traders were trying to persuade him to declare war against the settlers of the Red River, promising him all the goods and rum at Fort William, Sandy Lake, and Leech Lake as an incentive. Broken Tooth said that he would not agree to war until he had orders from British officials rather than the merchants of the Northwest Company.

In the summer of 1816 Broken Tooth journeyed to far off Drummond's Island on Lake Huron to visit the British high command. During a council with Colonel William McKay, Broken Tooth asked for presents befitting a man of his rank. The chief (according to Thomas McKenney) "was an orator of no small repute. Expert and ready in debate, his speeches were marked by shrewdness, ingenuity, and subtlety of argument, and by a simple brevity and force of expression."

> **...though I do not appear before you with a medal yet, I am descended from a great family who have always been considered good and faithful children to you, the Redcoats....I came from a great distance and...waited patiently in hopes of getting some of your milk [whisky] to drink, but I find you do not seem inclined to let me draw near your breast.**

Broken Tooth said that he was still in mourning for the death of his eldest son seven years before, and that this was the reason he was begging for "milk." The death of a relative was a common inducement for an Indian to seek alcoholic drink--for this would enable him to "weep" for his relations. Col. McKay refused drink on this occasion because, a short time previous, an Ojibway had gotten drunk and killed one of his own people.

Sources: Council, July 22, 1816, between Kattakabetay and Lt. Col. M'Kay, in McKay Papers, McCord Museum, Montreal, Canada; Thomas L. McKenney and James Hall, *The Indian Tribes of North America*, 3 vols., Frederick Webb Hodge, ed. (Edinburgh: J. Grant, 1933), 2:317.

FLAT MOUTH I

CHAPTER TWO

ADJUSTING TO THE AMERICANS, 1820-1836

"Give us a little milk, fathers, that we may wet our lips."

"We can live a great while upon a little, but we cannot live upon nothing."

BROKEN TOOTH July 16, 1820

IN THE SPRING OF 1820 General Lewis Cass, the governor of Michigan Territory, headed an expedition out of Detroit with the object of securing land for military posts at Sault Ste. Marie, Prairie du Chien, and Green Bay. He reached Fond du Lac on July 5 and Sandy Lake ten days later. Here he had a council with Broken Tooth (Katawabeda), the son of the renowned war chief, Biauswah, who had originally settled on Sandy Lake in a village site previously occupied by the Sioux. A military officer commented that Broken Tooth was "acknowledged to be the general leader of this part of the tribe as well as the others," and that he had raised himself "to his present advanced station by his superior eloquence alone and is said to be the first general ruler they ever have had." Young Henry Schoolcraft, a member of the expedition, recorded the chief's speech, and said that it was "one of the best specimens" that they had heard on their trip.

Father, we are glad you have come among us, to see how we live, and what kind of a country we inhabit, and to tell these things to our Great Father, the President.

Father, you see us here; we are poor; we want every thing; we have neither knives or blankets, guns or powder, lead or cloth, kettles or tomahawks, tobacco or whiskey. We hope you will give us these things.

Father, we are glad that the President has thought proper to send you among us; we are glad to see his flag wave upon this lake; we are his children, he is our father; we smoke the same pipe; we take hold of the same tomahawk; we are inseparable friends. It shall never be said that the Chippeways are ungrateful. Rather, depend on this, and take this pipe of peace as a pledge of our sincerity.

Father, we are of the race of strong men, of good warriors, and good hunters, but we cannot always kill game, or catch fish. We can live a great while upon a little, but we cannot live upon nothing.

Father, our wild rice is all eaten up; the buffaloes live in the land of our enemies, the Sioux; we are hungry and naked; we are dry and needy. We hope you will relieve us.

Father, the President of the United States is a very great man, even like a lofty pine upon the mountain's top. You are also a great man, and the Americans are a great people. Can it be possible they will allow us to suffer!

Source: Mentor L. Williams, ed. *Henry R. Schoolcraft, Narrative Journal of Travels* (Lansing: Michigan State College Press, 1953), 159, 486.

"I have been a long time acquainted with the British, but this day wish to quit them."

FLAT MOUTH July 1821

ALONG WITH AMERICAN military occupation of a post (to soon be called Fort Snelling), came Indian agent Lawrence Taliaferro, a young Virginian, who was a veteran of the War of 1812. He immediately began to have councils with chiefs of both the Dakota and Ojibway tribes at St. Peter's Agency. In 1821 he was visited by the renowned Pillager chief Flat Mouth, the Sandy Lake war chief Curly Head, and some 250 warriors. Flat Mouth wore a red British officers' coat of the type that English officials and traders gave to influential chiefs. In spite of his costume, the chief told the agent that he considered himself an American now:

> **My father, it is more than twenty years since I listened to the Americans. I have come to listen to your words--[I] will listen to you, and expect to carry back good words to the old and young men in my village.**
>
> **My father, I come down today, and you must not think hard of me that I have come into your house with a red coat on. I have been a long time acquainted with the British, but this day wish to quit them.**

The chief then turned his attention to the war raging between the Pillager Chippewas and the Sisseton Dakotas of Lake Traverse. He presented his pipe, with the comment that "it was rather longer than those presented by my chiefs, and it is clean...." He continued:

> **My father, all the Pillagers above listen to me, and they are numerous, and what you will say to me, as they have no fathers, I will say to them, and perhaps you will be pleased when you hear that they listen and do well.**

Taliaferro commented in his journal that Flat Mouth was "a great stickler for etiquette and is absolute among his band, and takes decidedly more authority than any chief of Indians I ever saw."

Source: Taliaferro Journal, May 10, and July 1821, Minnesota Historical Society, St. Paul.

"My friends, I wish to enjoy the same fireside with you...."

CURLY HEAD **July 1821**

CURLY HEAD (or Babesegundibay), was an influential Sandy Lake chief who took the lead to press his hunting parties southward into Dakota territory, particularly in the region where the Crow Wing River joins the Mississippi in central Minnesota. An Ojibway said of him: "He was a father to our fathers, who looked on him as a parent: his lightest wish quickly obeyed: his lodge was ever hung with meat; and the traders vied with each other who should treat him best: his hand was open, and when he had plenty, our fathers wanted not." Curly Head was also one of the leading war chiefs of his tribe, having distinguished himself in battle many times.

Curly Head accompanied Governor Cass to St. Peter's in 1820, and again visited the agent in 1821 along with Flat Mouth. Taliaferro called the chief "Kendosa." As very few speeches by this famous chief were ever recorded, the following is given from his council with Taliaferro and various Dakota chiefs regarding peace between the two tribes:

> **My friends, this is not the first time you have seen me here. I was here last year [1820] along with a chief of the Americans [Cass]. We talked but little then because but few of my young men came down. Since that time my nation has received good words from our father here, and as a great many of our best chiefs and warriors are now present, we hope to make peace.**
>
> **My friends, I wish to enjoy the same fireside with you, and if you receive this pipe of my nation and smoke on it, I will call down again next summer as I wish to hold my father tight by the hand.**

Taliaferro admitted great surprise when every chief and headman of the Dakotas who were present smoked Curly Head's pipe. Unfortunately, this popular Ojibway chief died following the government-sponsored peace council at Prairie du Chien in 1825. Just before he expired on the shores of Lake Pepin, he left his band in charge of his pipebearers--the two later famous brothers, Strong Ground and Hole-in-the-Day.

Sources: Henry R. Schoolcraft, *Information Respecting the History, Condition, and Prospects of the Indian Tribes of the United States*, Part 2 (Philadelphia: Lippincott, Grambo and Company, 1852), 161-62 (this section contributed by William Warren); Taliaferro Journal, May 10, and July 1821.

"They all talked of peace, but still...the Sioux continue to make war upon us."

BROKEN TOOTH **circa Summer 1822**

ALTHOUGH IT WAS A GREAT HARDSHIP to the Ojibways of the west, many of their chiefs still visited their agent, Henry R. Schoolcraft, at distant Sault Ste. Marie. In 1822 Broken Tooth made the long trip from Sandy Lake to the agency. Schoolcraft referred to the chief as the "venerable patriarch" of that region. Although Broken Tooth was widely known as an orator, very few of his speeches were ever recorded. In his talk with Schoolcraft he pronounced himself "a friend and advocate of peace." Unfortunately, Schoolcraft only recorded the substance of the chief's speech:

> **Broken Tooth discountenanced the idea of the Indians taking part in our wars. He said he was a small boy at the taking of old Mackinac [1763]. The French wished him to take up the war-club, but he refused. The English afterwards thanked him for this, and requested him to raise the tomahawk in their favor, but he refused. The Americans afterwards thanked him for this refusal, but they did not ask him to go to war. "They all talked of peace," he said, "but still, though they talk of peace, the Sioux continue to make war upon us. Very lately they killed three people."**

Broken Tooth's almost humorous characterization of the whites' policy toward the Indians in war time, prompted Schoolcraft to comment in his journal: "The neutral policy which this chief so early unfolded, I have found quite characteristic of his oratory, though his political feelings are known to be decidedly favorable to the British government." The chief only had about six more years to live, and it is doubtful that he ever sought any kind of help from British authorities. Many of the Indians, however, felt that the British were more generous in their presents to them than the Americans.

Source: Henry R. Schoolcraft, *Personal Memoirs* (Philadelphia: Lippincott, Grambo and Company, 1851), 293-94.

"Where do they get these things? From the Americans...."

SHINGABAOSSIN April 1823

SHINGABAOSSIN, OR STONE IMAGE, was the leading chief of the Ojibway bands at Sault Ste. Marie, and was considered by some as the first chief of the entire Ojibway nation. He was a very impressive man both in character and in appearance. Schoolcraft described him as "deliberate and thoughtful in mind--a man of policy, as well as bravery," and that "he was early sensible that the prosperity of his nation depended upon peace, and an assiduous attention to their ordinary occupations." While a youth, Shingabaossin had fought the Sioux several times, and was in the battle of St. Croix Falls in 1783. He had four wives and fathered some twenty children.

Due to the chief's close proximity to the Schoolcraft agency, he was undoubtedly more prone to pick up pro-American sentiment than his counterparts to the west. He, in fact, became a leading pro-American advocate in his tribe. On one occasion Schoolcraft recorded one of the chief's speeches in this regard:

> I have told you your Great Father is powerful and kind. If you look around, you will see that within a very few years he has sent his soldiers to build forts at Green Bay, at Tipisagee [Prairie du Chien], St. Peter's [referring to Fort Snelling], & Council Hills on the Missouri, where he feeds & clothes a great many people. It is not a year since he established this last post, & one at Sagana [Saginaw]. Is not this an evidence of his strength?
>
> When the British King wishes any of your lands, he puts his foot upon them, and says it is mine! He holds no treaty with you to buy it, nor does he pay you for it. But when your American Father wants your lands, he sends some of his civil chiefs to buy it, and to agree with you on the price of it. Is not this an evidence of his justice?
>
> Look at your brothers, the Saganaws, the Ottoways, the Pottawottamies, the Menominies & the Foxes! Do they not every year receive large sums of money from him? This is for the lands they have sold. Whenever your American Father has sent soldiers, he has sent an agent to see to your wants, to feed you when you are hungry, to clothe you when you are naked, and to give you drink when you are thirsty. Is this not evidence of his kind big heart?
>
> Look among your brothers, who are under the American government. Have they not plenty? You go sometimes to visit them. Have you not seen that they have horses, and cattle, guns and traps, fine blankets and clothes, and every thing else to make them happy? Where do they get these things? From the Americans....

Shingabaossin was also active in spreading his doctrine: he attended the Indian peace council sponsored by the Americans at the distant Prairie du Chien in 1825, and also spoke his pro-American sentiments at the treaty council held at Fond du Lac in 1826.

Source: Schoolcraft, *Literary Voyager*, 16-17, 29-30.

"The Great Spirit listens, and all the sky listens, to your charity in coming here to secure us in our lands."

SINGLE MAN and LOON'S FOOT August 1825

DUE TO CONTINUING HOSTILITIES between various tribes of the northwest, the government sent Governor Lewis Cass and.Colonel William Clark to council with the chiefs and headmen of all the tribes in the region. This great gathering was held in August 1825 at Prairie du Chien--or Tipisaga, as the Ojibways called it. Many Ojibway chiefs attended along with agents Schoolcraft and Taliaferro. They were anxious to have their land boundaries established by the government and to have their feud with the Sioux ended. Broken Tooth commented in this regard: "The Great Spirit listens, and all the sky listens, to your charity in coming here to secure us in our lands." Broken Tooth's son, Loon's Foot, or Mongazid, was also present as a representative of the Fond du Lac Ojibway bands. Schoolcraft referred to him as "a noted speaker, and jossakeed, or seer"--or in other words, an Ojibway medicine man. He had apparently married into the Fond du Lac band, and, as he told Schoolcraft, his influence had increased as one of the older chief's had declined. Loon's Foot boasted that of the 220 people at Fond du Lac, fifty-four were hunters, and they killed 994 bears in one year. At the council, the young chief spoke of his joy at the prospects of peace:

> **When I heard the voice of my Great Father [Colonel Clark] coming up the Mississippi Valley calling me to this treaty, it seemed as a murmuring wind. I arose from my mat where I sat musing, and hastened to obey it. My pathway has been clear and bright. Truly, it is a pleasant sky above our lands this day. There is not a cloud to darken it. I hear nothing but pleasant words. The raven is not waiting for his prey. I hear no eagle cry, "Come, let us go. The feast is ready; the Indian has killed his brother!"**

Also present was the young war chief of the St. Croix (or Snake River) Ojibways, Single, or Lone, Man (Piajick). He defined his land claims, giving the boundaries in terms of lakes and rivers (as all the chiefs did during the council). He also said:

> **My fathers: look at my mouth how it speaks, and my heart how it beats, and see if I tell you the truth.... This is the land I claim for myself and my children. Hereafter you will never hear of any bad clouds on it: it shall always be blooming and sunshine, and peace will reside there. My fathers--you see I appear young in years, but I do not speak altogether of my own mind, but listen to the words of the collected chiefs.**

The high hopes of the council were dashed within two years, when the Sioux attacked a number of Ojibways near Fort Snelling in May 1827. From then on peace agreements had to be looked upon with some skepticism. Despite the defining of land boundaries on paper, hunters of both tribes often pursued game into the other tribe's territory and conflict resulted.

Source: *Niles Register* (Washington), Nov. 19, 1825. Information on Loon's Foot in Schoolcraft, *Personal Memoirs*. 297-98.

"Give us a little milk, fathers, that we may wet our lips."

SHINGABAOSSIN and GREAT BUFFALO **August 2, 1826**

THE AMERICAN GOVERNMENT was greatly interested in investigating rumors of copper deposits on Ojibway lands. In the summer of 1826 Lewis Cass and Indian Superintendent Thomas L. McKenney held a council with the tribe at Fond du Lac on the western corner of Lake Superior. Cass told the chiefs frankly that the Great Father wanted "to take such copper as he may find" --in return the Ojibways would receive goods. Shingabaossin of the Sault bands put up no resistance to this statement as can be seen by the following speech. Ojibway historian William Warren later claimed that the chief only meant to "tickle the ears of the commissioners and gain their favor," as he "was too much imbued with the superstition prevalent...which prevents them from discovering their knowledge of mineral and copper boulders to the whites." Some doubt remains as to whether or not this was the case as the chief seems to have tried to persuade the leaders to expose whatever copper they knew about:

> **My brothers, take notice. Our Great Father has been at much trouble to make us live as one family, and to make our path clear. The morning was cloudy. The Great Spirit has scattered those clouds. So have our difficulties passed away.**
>
> **My friends, our fathers have come here to embrace their children. Listen to what they say. It will be good for you. If you have any copper on your lands, I advise you to sell it. It is of no advantage to us. They can convert it into articles for our use. If any one of you has any knowledge on this subject, I ask you to bring it to light.**

Great Buffalo (Kechewaishke) was another of the chiefs who responded to the commissioners, however, he disregarded the copper issue. This chief, from La Pointe, was the grandson of chief Audaigweos, who was the head of the Loon totem. Born in about 1755, he signed the 1825 peace treaty at Prairie du Chien, and on this occasion, looked for real assistance from the American government, as well as a little "milk" --meaning whiskey:

> **I am put here as a speaker....our compassion is strong for our women and children....And we are now here to see what you will do for us. We offer you our pipe.**
>
> **You, fathers, look to the Great Spirit in the sky and under the earth. You are strong to make your young men obey you. But we have no way, fathers, to make our young men listen, but by the pipe....You have many children. But your breasts drop yet. Give us a little milk, fathers, that we may wet our lips.**

Source: Thomas L. McKenney, *Sketches of a Tour to the Lakes* (Minneapolis: Ross and Haines, Inc., 1959), 458-62.

"...look at your floor, it is stained with the blood of my people...."

STRONG GROUND May 29, 1827

CONFIDENT IN THE PEACE that had been made with the Sioux in 1825, the three chiefs, Flat Mouth, Strong Ground, and Hole-in-the-Day, and a number of their people visited Fort Snelling in late May 1827; they camped outside of the fort's walls in three lodges. On the evening of May 28 they were visited by a party of Sioux, whom they hospitably entertained. However, just after parting company, the Sioux maliciously fired their guns into the crowded Ojibway lodges. Hole-in-the-Day was wounded in the breast, and his daughter was mortally wounded in the groin; another Ojibway was killed outright. Colonel Josiah Snelling gave shelter to the Ojibways inside the walls of the fort, no doubt being embarrassed by the shootings. Strong Ground, the elder brother of the bleeding Hole-in-the-Day, castigated the officer in the following speech:

> **Father, you know that two summers ago, we attended a great council at Prairie du Chien, where by the advice of our white friends we made a peace with the Sioux. We were then told that the Americans would guarantee our safety under your flag. We came here under that assurance.**
>
> **But father, look at your floor, it is stained with the blood of my people, shed under your walls. I look up and see your flag over us. If you are a great and powerful people, why do you not protect us? If not, of what use are all these soldiers?**

Snelling decided to placate the wronged Ojibways by turning over several of the Sioux offenders to them, to do with as they pleased. The Ojibways turned the Sioux loose adjacent to the fort, but then shot them down as they tried to make their escape--they were then scalped and mutilated. The following day, two more Sioux received similar treatment.

Source: Speech of Strong Earth (or Strong Ground), May 30, 1827, in Josiah Snelling Journal, MHS. See also, Mark Diedrich, *The Chiefs Hole-in-the-Day of the Mississippi Chippewa* (Minneapolis: Coyote Books, 1986), 4.

"....your councils gave peace to our bleeding lands."

HOLE-IN-THE-DAY July 16, 1827

AS A RESULT OF THE SIOUX attack on the Ojibways at Fort Snelling, Chief Hole-in-the-Day's daughter died. The chief, himself, recovered from his wounds, but was contemplating suicide due to depression over the loss of his daughter. Finally, however, he visited agent Taliaferro and said that he would not blacken his face--as was the Ojibway custom when in mourning. He explained that, although he was grief-stricken, he realized that his people had received many benefits by listening to Taliaferro's advice and he did not want to jeapordize his people's relationship with the Americans:

> **My father, when I first came to this country, and it is now a long time..., you took me by the hand and you see by my coming here every year that I have been pleased with your councils and treatment. I am not like many of my nation who carry two tongues. You are the man who first caused the roads to be cleared that my nation and the Sioux might meet at your house and enjoy but one fireside.**
>
> **My father, for a long time my nation used to visit the British, and our fathers, the Americans, on the lakes; every time they returned home something bad would happen. They appeared to have no ears to listen then, but would go to war. But since you hoisted your flag and this fort was built, they changed their road and came down to see you and have been good children. My father, your voice was heard throughout all our bands, and your councils gave peace to our bleeding lands. You made us bury our warclubs and we were happy.**

The chief, however, then expressed great shock when Taliaferro told him that the Ojibways should no longer look upon him as their agent, but rather would have to go to see Schoolcraft at the Sault. The chief replied: "What shall we do now? Like a dog we are driven from one door to find another." The Ojibways, for years afterwards, complained that they had no "father" in their own country.

Source: Taliaferro Journal, July 16-17, 1827.

"...I have suffered more since that time than any other person in my nation."

HOLE-IN-THE-DAY May 8, 1829

HOLE-IN-THE-DAY was a leading peace advocate among the Mississippi Ojibway, but during the late 1820s he suffered the loss of many relatives at the hand of the Sioux. In addition, his father died after the 1825 treaty council, as did his wife, and in the spring of 1829 a son of his died. His father-in-law, the great chief Broken Tooth, passed away in 1828. The chief appeared at the St. Peter's Agency in May 1829 with his face blackened. Referring to this custom of Ojibway mourning, Henry Lewis wrote in 1848: "The bereaved person takes a piece of wood, burns it to charcoal, and blackens his face, chest, and hands with it every morning until the whole piece has been used up. Not once during this time does he wash himself." The chief told Taliaferro of a recent attack made upon his people by the Mdewakanton Dakota, and that he had almost been killed by his own warriors for preventing them from retaliating:

> **My father, you know I have suffered more since that time than any person in my nation. You see I cannot keep my face clean. As fast as it is washed, I am compelled to black it again. But my heart toward you is the same. My father's bones sleep by your house. My daughter [lies] at the [St. Anthony] Falls near the grave of my uncle-- my wife lies at the mouth of Sauk River and a few days past I buried my son.**
>
> **My father, I can speak my mind and need not be ashamed for I have not harmed any man....I have done all I could to prevent war to let you see I listen to your good councils. You have done a great deal of good for my nation and your friendship for our people induces me to keep my hands clean. I called on my father expecting to hear good news from the Great Father as we wish still to have but one fireside with the Sioux.**

Sources: Taliaferro Journal, May 8, 1829; Henry Lewis, *The Valley of the Mississippi Illustrated*, Bertha L. Heilbron, ed. (St. Paul: Minnesota Historical Society, 1967), 118.

"I have sought death in battle, but have not met it."

FLAT MOUTH July 1832

IN THE SUMMER OF 1832 Henry R. Schoolcraft led an exploring expedition through northern Minnesota to find the source of the Mississippi River and to check on Ojibway affairs. At Leech Lake, he visited the Pillager chief Flat Mouth, who was greatly upset over the recent death of his son in a fight with the Sioux. The chief went on to relate the number of incidents of war that had broken the peace since the treaty of 1825. He said that, for himself, he had been in twenty-five fights with the Sioux during the course of his lifetime, but had not suffered even one wound. Schoolcraft wrote down the chief's speech, describing him as being about five feet and nine or ten inches in height, erect and stout, but "somewhat inclined to corpulency." At one point, the chief lifted up four silver medals smeared with vermillion. He said:

> Take notice, they are bloody. I wish you to wipe off the blood. I am unable to do it. I find myself irretrievably involved in a war with the Sioux. I believe it has been intended by the Creator that we should be at war with this people.
>
> I am not satisfied with the result of the last war party. My warriors are not satisfied. They are brave men. It is to them I owe success, and not to myself. Both they and I have heretofore looked for help where we did not find it (meaning the American government). We are determined to revenge ourselves. If the United States does not aid us, I have it in mind to apply for aid elsewhere (the British government).
>
> My warriors are in a restless state. I have sent my pipe and invitations to my friends around, to continue the war. Circumstances control me. I cannot avoid it. My feelings are enlisted deeply in the contest. When the enemy killed my son, I resolved never to lay down the war club. I have sought death in battle, but have not met it. All I can now say is this, that perhaps I shall not lead out the next war party.

He despairingly added later, "When I think of the condition of my people, I can hardly refrain from tears. It is so melancholy that even the trees weep over it."

Source: Henry R. Schoolcraft, *Schoolcraft's Expedition to Lake Itasca*, Philip P. Mason, ed. (East Lansing: Michigan State University Press, 1958), 54-56.

"The weight of these falsehoods can no more be lifted than a heavy rock."

MAJIGABO, STRONG GROUND, and BUFFALO   August 20, 1836

WHEN JOSEPH N. NICOLLET visited Leech Lake on August 20, 1836 to do a topographical survey of the region, he found the Ojibway headmen anxious to condemn American officials for wrongs committed against them by the Sioux-- in particular the recent killing of an Ojibway who was beaten to death. With translation by Joseph Montrelle (an Ojibway mixedblood, fur company employee), Majigabo made an impassioned speech to the French cartographer. He said that the whites had promised that the Sioux murderers would be punished, but they had not been. He then asked Nicollet to relay his words to Lawrence Taliaferro:

> **The weight of these falsehoods can no more be lifted than a heavy rock. My father, my heart mourns the loss of our warriors slaughtered by the Sioux. Were I to lose ten pigs I would be afflicted with grief. If a native lost ten pigs you would put in prison him who stole them. How can you expect us to stand still when those promises you made to us have yet to be fulfilled?**
>
> **Behold the size of this lake. To fill it with presents would be no compensation for the loss of our men killed by the Sioux. My father, you have contempt for your own heart when you speak falsehoods. I believed the things you said. My father, it occurs to me that perhaps your interpreter [Scott Campbell] changes the words you pronounce. You raised your finger toward the sky as you spoke, indicating thereby that God was a witness to what you said. It was understood the commander [Major John Bliss] was speaking the truth [when he said that the first one who killed would be seized and delivered to the Chippewas to do with what they will.]**

Nicollet then asked why the Ojibways hated the Americans. Strong Ground replied:

> **Yes, we hate them. Because wherever they establish military posts to protect the natives, they keep them like dogs. Because for the slightest folly we commit, they drive us under the ground (put us in prison), whip us with rope, tie cords around our neck and hang us. Our fathers always said they would love to see the French from France again, they who discovered this land and were good to us. We long for the French of the other shore, that they may prevent our young ones from exterminating the Americans.**

Buffalo, a Leech Lake chief, made the following humorous comments about Major Bliss:

> **I was convinced my father was a man; he had indeed many people in his fort; and also when I was in St. Peter, he unbottoned his breeches for his needs, and I did see that he was like us, that he had that which makes a man. Now, I dig up my hatchet again. I want my Great Father to be aware of it. We do not know on whom we can rely.**

Source: Martha C. Bray, ed. *The Journals of Joseph N. Nicollet* (St. Paul: Minnesota Historical Society, 1970), 77-83.

"We shall not surrender our land, not until every one of the warriors you see around me has been killed."

FLAT MOUTH September 10, 1836

LIKE HIS FELLOW CHIEFS, Flat Mouth was eager to give a recitation of his complaints against the seemingly indifferent American authorities. He made a lengthly speech to Nicollet at Otter Tail Point on Leech Lake in September, 1836. Translation was made by Francis Brunet, a trader. After complaining of the high prices the Ojibways paid to American traders, he said:

> **Of the Americans we hear no more than of the wind that passes by without stopping, leaving but a chill in our midst. Much is said of those soldiers who will run, nay fly, to our help. But never do we see them. Blood is shed before mine eyes; I see it is not that of the beasts of the forests, but that of my young ones, and yet we cannot avenge those crimes committed against us. We are endlessly told to bury the war hatchet, and if we dig it up we are threatened with rods, and ropes, or with being placed under the ground....**
>
> **Thus the Americans plan to treat us as they treat their black people. They do not come to see how we are in our homes, to find out about us, to help us as the French used to do, as the English used to do, and still do. I know why they do not come. It is because we are poor. But when they shall be poor as we are, then they shall come to take our land, not to till it with us, but to drive us west. We shall not go west! We shall not sell! We shall not surrender our land, not until every one of the warriors you see around me has been killed.**

The chief continued on for some time, and finally said pathetically that although the whites called him a chief, he did not consider himself to be one--"If I were a good chief, I would have saved my country from the predicament in which we find ourselves."

Source: Bray, *Journals of Joseph N. Nicollet*, 112-17.

CHAPTER THREE

THE HOLE-IN-THE-DAY ERA, 1837-1850

"If I am a chief, then my word is law...."

''Oblivion shall cover the past, and from this day we will be brothers.''

HOLE-IN-THE-DAY circa Spring 1837

DESPITE HOSTILITIES between the Sioux and Ojibway, Hole-in-the-Day, and his brother Strong Ground (who lived with their bands in the Crow Wing area), tried to maintain friendly relations with the Lac qui Parle Wahpeton Dakota. During the winter of 1836-37, the two groups hunted together in friendship. Later, the Ojibways parted company with the Dakotas, leaving a few of their friends and relations to continue hunting. Three days later, Hole-in-the-Day received word that his stepson, nephew, and cousin, had been killed by the Sioux. The chief was outraged and gathered up a large war party. He was about to attack the Wahpeton camp at Sauk Lake (near Sauk Centre, Minnesota), when he was convinced by his brother and his head soldier, White Fisher, to have a council with the Sioux. Hole-in-the-Day finally agreed to this proposition, and a council was subsequently held. The chief, at least at the time, firmly committed himself to keeping the peace, regardless of extreme provocation:

> All nations, although they still retain the practice of war, as for me, I now abandon it forever. I hold the Big Knives [the Americans] firmly by the hand. To them I look for protection. If you strike me twice, even thrice, I will not revenge--I will not look at it. We will render no aid to others in war. You shall not and I will not. From Pine Island to the place called Charged-upon-in-the-Night, the earth shall be wet no more. Over this extent of country we will hold on firmly to this pipe--you shall hold at the bowl and we will hold at the stem of this pipe, which shall remain in your keeping.
>
> On account of injuries received from you, we did determine your destruction. If you had visited us last winter, no matter how much you might have been disposed for peace, nor how great your numbers, not one of you would have escaped to bear the news of destruction to your wives and children. We would have butchered you, because white men advised us to do so; and besides, we have been informed by our friends, the Mdewakantonwans, that you intended treacherously to murder us; therefore, we would not have spared a solitary individual of you. Oblivion shall cover the past, and from this day we will be brothers. We will henceforth live in peace. The gods shall witness between us.

After the council, an arrangement was made for the Ojibway to hunt in the "Big Woods" on Sioux land; for this privilege they agreed to pay the Wahpetons a large quantity of sugar, a keg of powder, and some lead and tobacco. Payment was to be made at a rendevous location thirty-five miles northeast of Lac qui Parle in the spring of 1838. Hole-in-the-Day then arose and said, "In the name of the Great Spirit this peace shall be forever." He concluded by asking a missionary-taught Dakota to record his speech and the agreement they had made.

Sources: *Minnesota Chronicle and Register* (St. Paul), May 4 and June 3, 1850; Mary Eastman, *Dahcotah, or Life and Legends of the Sioux Around Fort Snelling* (New York: Arno Press, 1975), 192-94.

"We will be friends while we live and meet in that good place and be friends after we die."

LITTLE SIX May 1837

LITTLE SIX, OR SHAGOBE, was an Ojibway chief of the Snake River and St. Croix River bands (not to be confused with the Sioux chief Little Six, or Shakpaydan.) He met Joseph N. Nicollet in the fall of 1836, as the latter was mapping out the land of the Ojibways. Little Six aided Nicollet on a journey to Leech Lake, and also gave him an account of the secrets of the Ojibway medicine ceremony. The following spring, Six asked the missionary, William Boutwell, to pen the following to his French friend:

> **My friend, I think of you so much. I shake hands with you. I send these bear claws, which I take from my heart, that you may remember me.**
>
> **When I was young, I loved what I send you. When I was young, I dreamed if I kept this little animal's skin I should live long, and now I send it to you that you may remember me. We will be friends while we live, and meet in that good place and be friends after we die. I wish you to send me another shell by [Francis] Brunette such as you gave me last fall. Write me by Brunette that I may hear from you yourself. I am afraid I shall not be able to pay my credit [from a fur trader] if I don't hunt this spring or else I would come and see you before you leave.**
>
> **The last time I saw you I was poor. I am still poor now. I have not tobacco to fill my pipe. I shall still look for what you promised me in a small box.**

Nicollet felt very warmly about the chief, and stated in his reply: "My friend, I remember all things; I cannot forget. I have sent you something to fill your pipe, and as soon as the steamboat arrives I will not forget to fulfill all, and keep even friendship forever between us."

Source: Bray, ed. *Journals of Joseph N. Nicollet*, 19-20.

"Once I thought myself among the bravest of the brave...."

BIAJIG June 1837

BIAJIG was chief of the Lake Pokegama Ojibway band in the 1830s and early 1840s. Through the labors of missionary Frederick Ayer, the chief was converted to Christ and baptized. Ayer wrote his mission board that "the change in the chief" was "truly wonderful," and that "the songs of Zion" were heard daily in his lodge. Although the chief's life was threatened by traditionalists in his band, Biajig gave up all of the paraphenalia of the Ojibway religion. He told Ayer:

> **Formerly I thought myself very great. I fancied myself a manito [a spirit]. I was so wise. But now I think myself of no more consequence than the dirt on this floor. Once I thought myself among the bravest of the brave, but now...while reflecting upon my sins, I throw myself upon my knees weeping like a child, but can say nothing. Once I trusted in my idols and medicine; but now I trust only in Jesus.**

Sources: Frederick Ayer to David Greene, June 12, 1837, L. H. Wheeler to Greene, March 22, 1843, American Board of Commissioners for Foreign Missions (ABCFM) Papers, microfilm copies in Minnesota Historical Society, St. Paul. By 1844 Biajig's son-in-law, Bwanance (Boinance), was a chief of the band (along with Shineyah.)

"My father, what has happened to you? Have you cut off your breasts...?"

SINGLE MAN, MAJIGABO and FLAT MOUTH July 1837

IN THE SUMMER OF 1837, Commissioner Henry Dodge, the governor of Wisconsin Territory, met with the Ojibway chiefs at Fort Snelling to negotiate the sale of their land east of the Mississippi River. The chiefs of the various bands began to arrive from their villages in northern Wisconsin and Minnesota. Single Man (of the St. Croix Ojibways) expected that the commissioner would be generous with presents, commenting: "My father, what has happened to you? Have you cut off your breasts, that you cannot suckle your children. If you did so, it would render them more pliant and ready to yield to your wishes." Dodge soon asked the chiefs for the land cession, and on July 27, Majigabo, or Great Speaker, of the Pillager Ojibways, spoke for the assemblage of chiefs; they proved to be exceedingly willing to please their Great Father (Of course, they always expected that the government, in return, would be generous to them.)

> **My father, take the land you ask from us. Our chiefs have good hearts. Our women have brought the half-breeds among us. They are poor, and we wish them to be provided for. They are here, and have left many of their children behind them. We wish to divide with them all. This is the decision of the chiefs. Since we have met here this morning we have fully made up our minds to comply with your wishes....We will hold firmly [to] what you give us that nobody may get it from us.... We do not wish to disappoint you and our Great Father beyond the mountains in the object you had in coming here. We therefore grant you the country you want from us....**

On the following day, however, Flat Mouth qualified their acceptance, saying that they wanted the privilege of making maple sugar and fishing rights on the ceded lands:

> **It is hard to give up the land. It will remain and cannot be destroyed, but you may cut down the trees, and others will grow up. You know we cannot live deprived of lake and rivers. There is some game on the land yet, and for that we wish to remain upon it. Sometimes we scrape the trees and eat the bark. The Great Spirit above made the earth and causes it to produce that which enables us to live....We will wait to hear what you offer for the lands....**

On July 29 Dodge offered the Ojibways $800,000 plus $70,000 for debts to traders. The chiefs accepted this, and signed the treaty. Trader Lyman Warren later claimed that Taliaferro had exercised his influence to get Hole-in-the-Day and Flat Mouth to go along with the treaty. Flat Mouth expected that his band would partake in the annuities produced by the sale, but discovered the following year that they would not. And although Dodge told the chiefs that this sale was permanent, as late as the 1880s some Ojibways claimed that it was their understanding that they had sold only the timber on the ceded lands, not the land itself.

Sources: "Proceedings of a Council with the Chippewa Indians," *The Iowa Journal of History and Politics*, 9 (1911), 408-34; Lyman Warren statement, in Schoolcraft, *Memoirs*, 611; see Naganub letter to Gov. Lucius Hubbard, June 15, 1886, in *The Progress* (White Earth Agency), Feb. 18, 1888.

"If I am a chief, then my word is law, otherwise you might as well put this medal upon an old woman!"

HOLE-IN-THE-DAY July 1838

ON APRIL 11, 1838 Hole-in-the-Day and ten of his warriors went to the rendevous site with the Wahpeton Dakotas--but he went, not to trade goods for the privilege of hunting on Sioux lands, but to retaliate for wrongs committed against his people. Three lodges of Wahpetons greeted him and gave a feast in their honor, but afterwards Hole-in-the-Day and his warriors rose up and killed and mutilated their hosts. Almost everyone was killed, except for one woman who escaped and another who was taken captive by the chief.

About three months later, Miles Vineyard, who had been appointed subagent of the Upper Mississippi Ojibway (in response to many years' requests by those bands), went to recover the Sioux woman. A council was held at Little Falls in mid-July. Hole-in-the-Day came to the meeting with fifty warriors. Missionary Alfred Brunson, who was present, described the chief as "the dirtiest, most scowling and savage looking man in the crowd...." When it came time for him to speak, he arose from a pile of brush, according to Brunson, "as if shot by a gun," with "his eyes flashing like lightning," and with his "long hair literally snapping the air from the quick motion of his head." With Peter Quinn interpreting, he said that he was justified in attacking the Wahpetons because they had killed his relations "three times" at the same place; he added that the way in which the Sioux were killed was simply "the Indian way of warfare." In regard for demands that he give up his prisoner, he said:

> **My father! I don't keep this prisoner out of any ill will to you; nor out of ill will to my Great Father at Washington; nor out of ill will to these men (gracefully waving his hand back and round the circle); but I hate the Sioux. They have killed my relatives, and I'll have revenge. You call me a chief, and so I am, by nature as well as office, and I challenge any of these men (again waving his hand towards them), to dispute my title to it. If I am a chief, then my word is law, otherwise you might as well put this medal (showing the one he received from General Cass in 1825) upon an old woman!**

After retiring upon the brush pile for a time, the chief finally decided to relinquish the girl, saying, "My father, for your sake, and for the sake of these men, I'll give up the prisoner, and go myself and deliver her at the fort." However, the chief was persuaded not to make the trip as everyone knew that the Sioux would shoot him on sight!

Sources: Alfred Brunson, "Sketch of Hole-in-the-Day," *Wisconsin Historical Collections*, 5 (1869), 393-95; Miles M. Vineyard to Gov. Henry Dodge, July 16, 1838, Office of Indian Affairs (OIA), Letters Received (LR), St. Peter's Agency, roll 758, in MHS; Diedrich, *Chiefs Hole-in-the-Day*, 8.

"I am ready to die at any time."

HOLE-IN-THE-DAY circa July 1838

HOLE-IN-THE-DAY undoubtedly gave up his Sioux woman captive in order to mollify the Sioux and protect his people from probable retaliation. In addition, he composed a letter which he sent to the Wahpetons, explaining his actions and hoping plainly to deter their feelings of taking revenge:

> I have done what I was sorry for--but 4 times was I struck by you on the same ground where I found an opportunity to revenge the loss of my people. I look into your fort [Joseph Renville's trading post at Lac qui Parle] and know when you are at Lac qui Parle. I could go there, but I never did and will not--for war. I am sorry for what has happened but I could not help it. I return your relation with pleasure. I saved her life twice and would have killed the dog who had harmed her. I have fed and clothed her well. I wish if ever one of my relations should fall in to the hands of her husband, [that] they be saved and taken care of as I did of his wife.
>
> I am for peace. I promise never to strike another blow, and to kill the first of my nation who should dare to break the peace--provided the Sioux are willing to stop at once. I will never strike another blow on the Sioux, nor permit [it] to be done if I know it in time--if the Sioux will say they will not strike us.
>
> I have begged to go down and give myself up. I am ready to die at any time. I have done so once, and I know I can die but one time. Sooner or later this must take place, and a few short days makes no difference with me. I repeat that I am for peace--a permanent peace with you if you wish it on the terms I propose.
>
> Pagune Gizhik

The Wahpeton leaders responded with a letter of their own, saying that they did not believe him, and that his name was the name of a woman. The Wahpeton war chief, Rattling Cloud, later told Taliaferro: "We thought the Hole-in-the-Day a good man. He has changed, and hereafter you never can do anything with him. He is lost as a friend to peace." A Wahpeton war party went out against the Chippewas in October; they discovered a hunting party, which managed to escape, except for a pregnant woman, who was promptly killed. Earlier, in August, Hole-in-the-Day and a small party of men took the foolish risk of going down to Fort Snelling--one of the chief's comrades was killed by the Sioux, and he had to seek refuge in the fort.

Sources: Edmund C. Bray and Martha C. Bray, eds. *Joseph N. Nicollet on the Plains and Prairies* (St. Paul: Minnesota Historical Society, 1970), 278-79; Taliaferro Journal, June 23, August 2-3, 1838; Stephen Riggs to David Greene, October 1838, American Board of Commissioners for Foreign Missions Papers (ABCFM), MHS.

"The Indians' glory is passing away--they are as the setting sun!"

HOLE-IN-THE-DAY June 1845

DURING THE LATE-1830s and early 1840s, Hole-in-the-Day, largely on the basis of his unrelenting warfare with the Sioux, and his superior intellect and force of personality, became the leading Ojibway chief of the Mississippi bands. While he won great renown as a war chief, he was also firmly of the opinion that peace with the Sioux would have to be obtained before he could encourage his people to take up agricultural pursuits, and in general adapt to the white man's civilization. He, therefore, went to Fort Snelling in 1843 and made a treaty with the Sioux. He promised to back it up by bringing offenders among his people to justice.

Hole-in-the-Day's resolutions were tested in the spring of 1845, when the Sioux killed the Ojibway chief, Little Curly Head, and a member of Hole-in-the-Day's band retaliated. Hole-in-the-Day brought the man down to Fort Snelling, and called a council with the Mdewakanton Dakota chiefs of the vicinity. It was decided to call it even. A celebration then took place, with games and a feast. Then Hole-in-the-Day made the following address. Mary Eastman, wife of Fort Snelling captain Seth Eastman, was present, and commented of the chief: "Deeds of blood marked his course, yet were his manners gentle and his voice low. There was a dignity and a courtesy about his every action that would have well befitted a courier."

> **Warriors! it has been the wish of our Great Father that we should be friends; blood enough has been shed on both sides. But even if we preferred to continue at war, we must do as our Great Father says. The Indians' glory is passing away; they are as the setting sun; while the white man is as the sun rising in all his power. We are the falling leaves; the whites are the powerful horses that trample them under foot. We are about to return home, and it is well that nothing has happened to occasion strife between us. But I wish you to know that there are two young men among us who do not belong to my band. They are Pillagers, belonging to another band, and they may be troublesome. I wish you to tell your young men of this, that they may be on their guard.**

Sure enough, the very two Pillagers of whom the chief spoke, left Hole-in-the-Day's camp at St. Anthony Falls and shot and killed a Sioux near the fort. Word was sent to the chief of the killing, requesting him to give up the two killers, but Hole-in-the-Day could not find them. Instead, he gave up two of his own men to serve as hostages until the killers were brought in. However, the hostages were kept waiting for eighteen months before they were released. One, whose health had been extremely impaired during his confinement, died on the return to his home.

Sources: Eastman, *Dahcotah*, 95-102; *Minnesota Chronicle and Register*, May 4 and June 10, 1850.

"...when he died I took his place, and am consequently chief over all the nation."

HOLE-IN-THE-DAY (THE YOUNGER)   August 2, 1847

IN MAY 1847 the great chief Hole-in-the-Day, while hungover from a drinking bout, threw himself from a Red River ox cart and was critically injured. He told his son to take the Ojibways by the hand and "make them resemble the whites." Then he died and was buried at Little Falls, Minnesota. His son, known as "Boy" was but twenty years old at the time--he, himself, commented--"I was nothing but a mere foolish child. I knew nothing, and did not care about knowing anything." But with his father's last charge to him, he decided to fill his father's moccasins: "I meditated day and night upon what he said, and have done the best I could to promote the welfare of my people."

About two months later, Boy, along with the Mississippi chiefs and headmen, made the trip to Fond du Lac, where old Hole-in-the-Day had been expected for a treaty council, to sell land upon which the Winnebago tribe was to be located. The other chiefs of the nation were already present and had been discussing the news of Hole-in-the-Day's death--they spoke derogatorily of his son. However, Young Hole-in-the-Day's address to the council surprised everyone! It began his career as the foremost orator of the tribe. William Warren interpreted.

> **Our Great Father instructed you to come here, for the purpose of asking us to sell a large piece of land, lying on and west of the Mississippi River. To accomplish this you have called together all the chiefs and headmen of the nation, who to the number of many hundreds, are within the hearing of my voice: that was useless, for they do not own the land; it belongs to me. My father, by his bravery, took it from the Sioux. He died a few moons ago, and what belonged to him became mine. He, by his courage and perseverance, became head chief of all the Chippewas, and when he died I took his place, and am consequently chief over all the nation. To this position I am doubly entitled, for I am as brave as my father was, and through my mother I am by descent the legal heir to the position.**
>
> **Now, if I say sell, our Great Father will obtain the land; if I say no, you will tell him he cannot have it. The Indians assembled here have nothing to say; they can but do my bidding.**

On top of his declarations, Hole-in-the-Day demanded that the commissioners negotiate with him alone. Then, after he agreed to the treaty, he requested that all of the other chiefs sign it before him, that he would sign alone the following day, August 3. By this treaty a triangular section of land below Crow Wing and west to Long Prairie was ceded as a home for the Winnebagoes. The Mississippi bands were to receive $17,000, plus $1,000 annually for forty-six years.

Sources: Edward D. Neill, "History of the Ojibways," in Warren, *History of the Ojibway*, 497-98; *St. Paul Daily Press*, June 30, 1868; Diedrich, *Chiefs Hole-in-the-Day*, 15-16.

"Why make a treaty with us if our Great Father can alter it without our consent?"

HOLE-IN-THE-DAY (THE YOUNGER) July 25, 1848

ACTING UPON THE TREATY OF 1847, the government began to remove the Winnebago tribe from Iowa to Long Prairie, Minnesota. However, while they were enroute, Hole-in-the-Day learned that one of the articles of the treaty had been stricken out, in regard to having their annuity payments made to them on the Mississippi, rather than distant LaPointe. The chief quickly gathered up all of the bands in the region and faced off against the Winnebago procession at Sauk Rapids. Hole-in-the-Day told the Winnebago agent, Jonathan Fletcher, that he would not agree to the removal unless the government agreed to pay the Mississippi bands their annuities on the Mississippi as had been promised. He then dictated the following petition to be sent to the Great Father:

> **Father, we and our people live upon the waters of the Great River--we have been compelled to go to an island in the Great Lake [Superior] ; we have to travel, some of us, ten days, a part of the way in canoes, and a part of the way over a very rough and uninhabited country. When we reach the Great Lake we are without canoes, and are dependent upon the traders of the American Fur Company for a passage to LaPointe. This never costs less than two dollars each. Often we have been detained at Fond du Lac in consequence of high winds, until we were starved out and compelled to return, or until it was too late to get to the payment. When we have succeeded in reaching LaPointe (a barren island), we have received never over four dollars and fifty cents each in money....**
>
> **In crossing the Great Lake our lives were in danger. The provisions furnished us during payments last but a few days and we are usually kept on this island from twenty to forty days waiting for our payment....We are obliged to leave our women and children in the greatest destitution and misery for the term of two months, in order to get our payment. During this time they are obliged mostly to live on wild berries, and we find them starved and starving when we return from this long and arduous journey....**
>
> **We signed the treaty last summer upon Mr. [Henry M.] Rice giving us his word that we should have our rights. We have heard that we were to be disappointed and that our Great Father would not make his commissioners' words good. Why make a treaty with us if our Great Father can alter it without our consent? Why make children of us? We cannot understand why our treaty was altered without asking us--if that was right, our Great Father can take our lands without asking, or without price....**

With Fletcher's endorsement, Hole-in-the-Day's request was granted, and the government also allowed Fletcher's Winnebago agency to become responsible for the Mississippi Ojibway. Thus, Young Hole-in-the-Day proved his effectiveness in dealing with the government, and he consequently dominated Ojibway-white affairs until his death two decades later.

Sources: Jonathan Fletcher to T. Harvey, July 25, 1848, with Chippewa statement enclosed, OIA, LR, Winnebago Agency, roll 932; Diedrich, *Chiefs Hole-in-the-Day*, 20.

"All men that live have minds of their own, and had better settle their own affairs."

WILLIAM W. WARREN and HOLE-IN-THE-DAY June 1850

IN THE LATE WINTER OF 1849-50, the Mississippi Ojibways received two significant blows from the Sioux: the son of Chief White Fisher was killed and scalped on the Crow Wing River, and on April 2 a party of fifteen men and women received a similar fate on the Apple River. William Warren, an Ojibway mixed-blood, who was a government interpreter, and also a member of Hole-in-the-Day's band, wrote a warning to a St. Paul newspaper:

> **Mark me! that blood will not call for vengeance in vain. If the strong arm of the government will not interfere to punish the aggressors, there are still a few Chippewa warriors unmassacred, whose knives will soon open the veins of the murderers of their wives and children. Fear shall fall on the villages of the Sioux, and in two years, if the war is allowed to have free scope, their chiefs will be glad to sell the country.... They will even walk the streets of St. Paul with trembling steps, for we have boys among us that will tear off their scalps even there, and probably before this article reaches the press, a proof will have been given that my words will come to pass.**

Perhaps Hole-in-the-Day put Warren up to writing the letter, for on May 15, he and two companions, having hidden themselves in the Fountain Cave, just above St. Paul, ambushed and killed a Sioux man. By that time, the new territorial governor, Alexander Ramsey, had planned a peace council between the two tribes at Fort Snelling. On June 10 Hole-in-the-Day arrived at the fort with all of the Mississippi chiefs and about eighty warriors. On the following day, the Treaty of 1843 was read to the assemblage, and the chief commented that the Chippewas were never the first to violate it; he later went on to say:

> **My father, as you sent for me, I have come. I came at once for the reason I thought you would be here to enforce the treaty made by my father, Hole-in-the-Day, on this spot. I have always submitted to wrong for a long time. My father also did so.**
>
> **Respecting the sale by my father, Hole-in-the-Day, of lands once belonging to the Sioux, you know, my father, that by the treaty of Prairie du Chien, a boundary line was made between the Sioux and Chippewa lands. It was land we had conquered from the Sioux. The treaty of 1843 was afterwards made. The first man murdered after that treaty was my elder brother. We understand he was killed by one of Six's [or Shakopee's] band. There, my father, is a list of the wrongs the Chippewas have suffered since the treaty of 1843. It is signed by our chiefs, braves, and head men, and it is true.**

When an agreement eluded a committee of men appointed by each tribe to settle the matter, Hole-in-the-Day quipped: "All men that live have minds of their own, and had better settle their own affairs."

Sources: *Minnesota Chronicle and Register*, June 10, 1850; *Minnesota Pioneer* (St. Paul), June 13, 1850; Diedrich, *Chiefs Hole-in-the-Day*, 21.

CROSSING SKY

CHAPTER FOUR

THE SANDY LAKE DISASTER, 1850-1853

"...I blame him [Governor Ramsey] for the children we have lost...."

"Tell him I blame him for the children we have lost...."

FLAT MOUTH December 3, 1850

NEARLY 3,000 OJIBWAYS gathered at Sandy Lake to receive their annuities in the fall of 1850. However, the money did not arrive for two months. In the meantime, they were fed spoiled provisions of musty pork head, rotten corned beef, and bad flour. Before long, 150 people were dead. Although William Warren blamed the contractors for the disaster, Flat Mouth felt that Governor Ramsey was responsible, and therefore sent the following message to him through agent John S. Watrous:

> **I want you to write down the words I speak and carry them to him. Tell him I blame him for the children we have lost, for the sickness we have suffered, and for the hunger we have endured. The fault rests on his shoulders.**
>
> **Why were our goods not given to us at Crow Wing? Why were we brought here to be made a laughing stock among the other Indians? Tell him I blame him for this.... I told him last spring that we got nothing to eat from our Great Father when we came to the payment, but had to depend upon the charity of our fellow Indians to supply us. The Governor promised to feed us while here. He has not done it. We have been stealing all we have eaten from our fellow Chippewas; of this we have been accused and made a laughing stock thereby....**
>
> **My friend, it makes our hearts sore to look at the losses we have sustained while at Sandy Lake. You call us your children, but I do not think we are your children. If we were, we should be white. You are not our father and I think you call us your children only in mocking. The earth is our father and I will never call you so. The reason we call the earth our father is because it resembles us in color; and we call the sky our grandfather. We do not sell the ground to our Great Father. We gave it to him in order that he might follow our example and be liberal to us. I told the Governor at Crow Wing that we had not received an equivalent for our lands--that we wanted more. As much again as we got would not be too much. I expected to have seen him here. I should have called upon him to increase our annuity. When I saw him at Fort Gaines others heard what he said. He promised to get us more. Will he do it? If he will, let him add one half to our present payment. If he will do this, we will again come for our annuities; but if not, we will not come. Our people will not come if I tell them not to....I have great influence with the upper Indians, and when I put words into their hearts they are not soon forgotten nor lightly regarded....I call on you to double our payment next year. I do not blame our Great Father because we were so badly cheated in the sale of our lands. It was the traders' fault. He put honey on his lips to deceive us; and if our annuity cannot be doubled next year, we will not come for it....**

Source: Flat Mouth speech, Dec. 3, 1850, recorded by John Watrous, in Alexander Ramsey Papers, MHS.

"Many of them come to me and propose to fight the whites."

HOLE-IN-THE-DAY January 8, 1851

LIKE FLAT MOUTH, Hole-in-the-Day, too, wished to bring the disaster at Sandy Lake to the attention of the whites. He went down to St. Paul and arranged a meeting at the Presbyterian church, inviting all the members of the territorial legislature to come and hear him speak--he was but twenty-two years old, and had received no formal education, yet he proved his great oratorical ability on this occasion:

> **My friends, you see before you one who is like a child. You have all heard of my deceased father. Had he been allowed by the Great Spirit to live out the full term of existence allotted to mankind, you should have seen him in my place, speaking in behalf of his people.**
>
> **My friends, you see me here often. I come in behalf of my people, to speak to you of their poverty and sufferings, which you should be made to know....**
>
> **I request you to look back to the past history of my tribe, and you will see that we have always been the friends of the whites, but we have nevertheless suffered! Friends, I come to place things before your eyes, that you may all know the truth.**
>
> **You tell us that the Great Spirit has made all his children, red and white men all alike out of the earth, and that we are all equally his children. If this be true, why do not the whites treat us as friends and brothers?**
>
> **You tell us that the Great Spirit placed us on this earth to be friends and equals. Your red brothers believed you, and have yielded up to you their lands; to them the consequences are poverty, suffering, and starvation. Many of our people will not see the budding of the leaves of another spring. Though we have sold the greatest portion of our lands; we have gained nothing by it. We are poorer than ever. The more treaties we make, the more miserable we become. I could tell you many things to prove to you the truth of what I say.**

The young chief went on to relate his people's experience at Sandy Lake. He warned that a "crisis" had come, and if nothing was done his people's friendship toward the whites would turn to hatred. He requested a new agent, and hoped that his complaints would reach the Great Father's ear. He continued:

> **I consider it a duty I owe to myself and to you to inform you that the hearts of my people are bad and are aching. They are starving! Many of them come to me and propose to fight the whites. It is getting to be difficult to keep my young men within bounds. I am afraid they will soon commit some foolish act which will forever break our friendship.**
>
> **They are driven to extremities. Death is on every side, and in the minds of our young men, one death is as good as another. They wish to throw themselves away. They are like some poor animal driven into a hole and condemned to die....**

The citizens of St. Paul agreed to take up a collection to alleviate the situation.

Sources: *Minnesota Democrat* (St. Paul), Jan. 21, 1851; Diedrich, *Chiefs Hole-in-the-Day*, 21-22.

"We are pushed on to death without being allowed a hearing."

HOLE-IN-THE-DAY June 30, 1851

ON TOP OF THE BOTCHED UP PAYMENT at Sandy Lake, which resulted in the deaths of over one hundred Ojibways, Governor Ramsey and agent John Watrous began a removal of the Wisconsin Ojibways in the summer of 1851 ostensibly to the very same site--Sandy Lake. Some 4,000 Indians were supposedly going to live in that area, where the soil was poor and the country was destitute of game. Some observers blamed Ramsey for selecting that location. Hole-in-the-Day, who worked to oppose and frustrate the removal, blamed Watrous for not getting their complaints through to Washington. "For that reason," he said, "I follow the custom of the whites, and have my words burnt on paper that all may know my mind; and some one may feel interest enough in our fate to repeat my words to our Great Father," referring to a letter of his published in a St. Paul newspaper. In it he argued against the removal of the Ojibways to Sandy Lake:

> This season our tribe is being gathered to be again brought to Sandy Lake, their--graveyard. In case of refusal, threats are made of the consuming anger of their Great Father--his soldiers--loss of payments, &c. Promises of plenty to eat, large farms, &c., are made to induce them to come; but I see not a thing of all this. I see no adequate preparation to feed and support them in their new country. My people told me last fall to send them word when I saw that they could live here, but as many promises have been made and broken with us, we are learning not to believe till we see.
>
> I have sent my people word to remain where they are, for I can see nothing before them here but starvation and death. Sickness is already prevalent at Sandy Lake. Some corn has been taken there, but having been wet, it was sprouting out of the bags. For thus attending to my sacred duty to my people, and trying to prevent the death that desolated our wigwams last fall, I hear that our agent has requested the commanding officer to confine me in the guard house at Fort Ripley. What right he would have in thus doing, he only knows.
>
> I speak to my white brethren. I ask and demand of the whites that before they allow such an extreme measure to be taken with me, which will turn my friendship into gall and hatred, that I be allowed a fair and impartial hearing, and trial according to the custom of the whites. If I am guilty, I will not flinch from punishment. It will require no soldiers to take me--I will deliver myself up without murmur.
>
> It is not the wish of the Chippewas to break any treaty with our Great Father, though it may have been misinterpreted to us, and misunderstood. We do not wish to throw ourselves into the fire, by measuring our puny strength with his. On the contrary, we wish to remain under his protection. We hear that he has kindly made provision to help our people remove, and make farms to support them after removal. Let this be done under the management of people who know our wants and feel for our interests;

> people whom we can point out, and not, as it is, in the hands of selfish traders, and people who make money their only Great Spirit. Let this be done--let me but see that my people can live on my lands, and I will be the first to urge them to come; I will travel from village to village to induce them to obey the wishes of our Great Father. But as long as they are fed on false promises and rotten provisions, I shall consider it my duty to advise them to remain at home; for it is better that they should die there, than come here to die, incurring the same fate of the few who are barely able to support life from the resources of their poor country....
>
> We have always obeyed the slightest wish of our Great Father, and we have sacrificed our best interests to gain his good will. Never has he demanded our lands but we granted them at his own price. For this he should have pity on us. He should not trample us under foot and see us die off by hundreds, as we hear has been the fate of tribe after tribe of his more eastern red children....
>
> The Chippewas are poor; they have even no great trader at Washington [a reference to Henry Sibley] to speak for them to their Great Father. For this reason I am obliged to speak as I best may for my people. Though it may cost me my liberty, it is my duty, and I will continue to speak, and act also, till the wrongs of my people shall be righted.

Probably due in large part to Hole-in-the-Day's opposition, the removal was stopped, although some of the Indians were brought to Fond du Lac to receive their annuities. Even in this there seemed to be underhandedness, for William Warren charged agent Watrous of collaborating with the traders at that location to get the Indians in a place "where whiskey in any quantities could be procured...."

Sources: *Minnesota Democrat*, July 15 and December 10, 1851.

"Just as my father supported me, so that land yet supports me."

MOOSE DUNG **September 15 and 20, 1851**

IN THE FALL OF 1851, the U. S. government appointed the territorial governor of Minnesota, Alexander Ramsey, as a commissioner to treat with the Red Lake and Pembina bands. It wished to acquire a land cession from the Ojibways thirty miles in width on both sides of the Red River of the North, from the international boundary line with Canada, south to the Buffalo River. Ramsey, along with Hugh Tyler and Thomas Foster, arrived at Pembina by September 15 and had a council with a young chief named Moose Dung (Monsomo). As some of the more elderly chiefs were absent, Moose Dung was called upon by his people to speak for them. He rejected Ramsey's initial offer of a $30,000 "in hand" payment for the land, and $10,000 annually for twenty years, saying:

> **My father, all these around know I am not accustomed to say anything in this way; but I am now called here to speak, and I am not to be abused. The one who interrupted me just now has not told what land I own. I want to talk about that now.**
>
> **I do not see the minds of my friends around me. I think a great deal of the piece of land my father points to. Upon it is where my own father raised me, even up to the place you named [Buffalo River]. Just as my father supported me, so that land yet supports me. I love it---I love it, for I live by and on it.**

When Ramsey threatened to dissolve the council, the Ojibway said that they would talk among themselves and offer a counter proposition to Ramsey's offer. On September 20 Moose Dung addressed Ramsey again. He said that they wanted more money for their lands and permission to cross the land in order to hunt or war against the Sioux; they did not like the idea of the governor "building a fence to keep them back." Moose Dung presented a paper asking for $40,000 in hand and $20,000 annually. Ramsey congratulated the Ojibways for their bargaining ability, but said that they must sign the treaty for the original offer. Moose Dung conceded and said, "We have concluded to let you have our land for what you have written." He asked that the old, respected Pembina chief, Broken Arm, sign the documents.

Sources: Journal of U.S. Commissioner to Treat with Chippeway Indians of Pembina and Red Lake, Aug. 18 to Nov. 27, 1851, J. P. Bardwell to Luke Lea, Feb. 19, 1852, and Ramsey to Lea, Feb. 2, 1852, in OIA, Minnesota Superintendency, LR, roll 428, microfilm copy in MHS.

"We look to the ocean; we must be driven to its shores; perhaps we shall be drowned."

CROSSING SKY September 1851

CROSSING SKY was the son of Chief Big Mouth of the Sandy Lake Ojibway. When Big Mouth was killed by the Sioux in 1839, Crossing Sky became a chief. He vowed to avenge his father's death, and became a great warrior who fought in ten battles and earned twenty feathers. By 1851 he and his fellow chief, One Standing Ahead (Naganegabowh), took their bands and established a new village at Rabbit Lake. Due to the talk of removal by government officials, Crossing Sky led a delegation to St. Paul to talk to the commissioner of Indian affairs, Luke Lea. With John Johnson (or Enmegahbowh), the Episcopalian missionary, interpreting, the chief said:

> My father....Before I left my country every Indian gave me counsel, and told me what to say to you and to our Great Father, and when I return they will look to me for a reply. I come here to talk to you because I feel that I have done no wrong, and committed nothing evil, either against the whites or my own people. I have come a long way, and have been very anxious to see you, my father, and my Great Father. These wampums were present before many chiefs, and the words that I now speak are the words they wished me to say.
>
> Our people have become very much troubled, and very anxious in their minds, for fear that their Great Father is going to take away their lands; they look all about in every direction, and they look to the Canada side.
>
> We look around. We have no refuge, no shelter. We look to the ocean; we must be driven to its shores; perhaps we shall be drowned. Some of our chiefs have wished to go to Canada, and some have determined to die in their native land. They have great expectation from me, that I shall get a good reply from our Great Father.
>
> I am going to say a few words respecting payments. We were informed by our agent that we should be furnished a farmer, a blacksmith, and a teacher among our people. I have often asked for all these things....It is now almost fifteen years since we have received annuities, and all this time we have had no teacher. I am very anxious. Before the time comes that we shall be driven from our country, we wish to learn the ways of the whites....And about our timber I want to speak. Last winter I went down to ask the Governor about our timber, and I got no satisfactory answer. I wanted to get whitefolks to come into our country, and to put up sawmills in our country. We are anxious and ready to build, but we can't build without boards. I am weak and poor, truly weak; you have great strength. You can move great things. I leave this [the wampum] with you.

The commissioner said, that as long as the Chippewas remained scattered throughout their country, it would be impossible to grant them the improvements they desired.

Source: *Minnesotian* (St. Paul), September 24, 1851. Crossing Sky's Ojibway name is usually given in two different spellings--Iaskwekeshig and Mayzhuckegeshig.

"...I was among the Chippewa people, what Napoleon was among the French."

FLAT MOUTH March 1852

WILLIAM W. WARREN, the mixed-blood Ojibway, began to gather the traditions and historical narratives of his tribe in the 1840s. He spent alot of time with the venerable old chief of the Pillagers, Flat Mouth. This chief was unquestionably one of the greatest warriors and orators of his nation. According to his son, Flat Mouth was the son of a captive Sioux man and an Ojibway woman; he was later adopted by a Leech Lake chief in about 1793. On the basis of his natural talents Flat Mouth became a leader by the time that Pike visited Leech Lake in 1806. During this period, the chief traveled a great deal, was involved in numerous war expeditions, and had once visited the Gros Ventres (or Hidatsa) tribe on the Missouri.

During his March 1852 visit with Warren, and a newspaper reporter, he spoke of his dissatisfaction with a recent treaty made by the Pembina Ojibway; he felt that the government had taken land which his band depended upon for game. He said he was grieved to think that "now, when he is tottering on the brink of the grave, and has but a day to live, that the whites wish to wrest from him the lands far off, which he had intended to leave his children and his young men." He went on to reminisce and boast of his accomplishments:

> **When I was young, I was among the Chippewa people, what Napoleon was among the French. I was to them, as the tall oak is to the small trees that stand at its base. By my counsels all this surrounding country was conquered from the Sioux. The whole earth is indented by my warclub. But my whole history attests my friendship for my white brethren.**

When asked if he would fight the Sioux if they attacked his lodge at Leech Lake, the chief replied: "If when young and engaged against my enemies, I placed little value upon my life, how much less should I value it now when old, with but a day to live?"

Sources: *Minnesota Democrat* (St. Paul), March 17, 1852; Charles H. Beaulieu, "Origin of the Name given to Leech Lake...and Sketch of Flat Mouth...." unpublished manuscript, Clement H. Beaulieu Papers, MHS. One might wonder how Flat Mouth came to knowledge of Napoleon. The answer probably is that Joseph Nicollet was the main source. Nicollet, who visited Flat Mouth in 1836, writes: "I showed him a snuffbox... upon the lid of which was a full-length portrait of Napoleon at St. Helena. The chief took much notice of this portrait, and questioned me largely about this great warrior, whom he named *Naponeon*....He frequently asked me for the box; and contemplating it would say, 'Well, it is strange, on whatever side I turn it, the figure looks at me, and seems to say "thou art my brother warrior." ' "

"I find that my provision-bag is fast emptying--my dish is now often empty."

GREEN SETTING FEATHER September 14, 1852

IN THE SUMMER OF 1854 Isaac Stevens wrote to George Manypenny, the commissioner of Indian affairs, of his experience among the Red River Metis. He also spoke of his meeting with the Turtle Mountain Ojibway chief, Green Setting Feather (Wayshawwushkoquenabe). The chief bitterly resented the mass killing of the buffalo by the Metis. He presented Stevens with a copy of a speech he had given two years before at St. Joseph, which said:

> In time past, whenever I looked over my hunting grounds, I ever found a plenty with what to fill my dish, and plenty to give my children, but of late it is not so. I find that my provision-bag is fast emptying--my dish is now often empty; and what is the cause of this? Why was it not so in former times, when there were more Indians on the plains than there are now?
>
> The reason I find is this: it is none other but the children I once raised, that first proceeded from my own loins, that were once fed from my own hands, which child is the half-breed. The manner of his hunt is such as not only to kill, but also to drive away the few he leaves, and waste even those he kills.
>
> I also find that same child, in the stead of being a help to me, his parent, is the very one to pillage from me the very dish out of which I fed and raised him when a little child; and now having gained strength and grown to manhood, has become master of my own dish, and leaves me with the wolves and little animals to follow his trail and pick off the bones of his leaving; and if I wish to help myself out of my own foodbag, his hand and whip is raised on me, his parent.
>
> When I look at all this, my heart is pained within me. I now see my provisions all wasted. I am led to think that it is my Creator that puts it in my heart no more to allow this waste of animals he has given me; therefore, [I] look to him as my Father to help me to remove those that are eating up and pillaging my food from me. I have no bad feeling, and do not wish to use my strength. It is my food [that] I am looking at; I only wish to be master, and do as I please with what is my own. I now say, I hold back, and love, all of the Turtle Mountain. From it the half-breeds must keep, and stop on the place their father gave them at Pembina.

However, the chief could do little about the slaughter of the buffalo on the plains. Twice a year about one thousand Metis would roll onto the plains with their Red River ox carts, killing thousands of buffalo, trading furs and pemmican to the Hudson Bay Company, the Red River traders of the American Fur Company, and to buyers in St. Paul.

Source: Isaac Stevens to George Manypenny, Sept. 16, 1854, 33 Congress, 2 Session, *House Executive Document*, vol. 1, 1854-55 (serial 777), 397-401.

"Now I shall tell you how we met with our degradation."

HOLE-IN-THE-DAY **June 15, 1853**

THE WINNEBAGO TRIBE had been moved to Long Prairie, Minnesota, in the late 1840s, not only to free up Iowa lands for white settlement, but also to serve as a buffer between the Sioux and Chippewa. Ironically, trouble between the Winnebago and Chippewa threatened the arrangement. In the spring of 1853 two Ojibways were killed by Winnebagoes; the Winnebagoes feared Ojibway retaliation for the killings and began a tribal retreat down the Mississippi River. Hoping to prevent the tribe from abandoning its reservation and restore peace, territorial governor Willis A. Gorman quickly arranged a council between the two tribes (and a few Sioux chiefs) at Sauk Rapids.

In mid-June Hole-in-the-Day arrived with the usual contingent of Mississippi chiefs, including Berry Picker (the son of Broken Tooth), Feather's End, Big Wind, Attownh, Crossing Sky, Bad Boy, and Rice Maker; they were accompanied by agent David Herriman and interpreter Peter Roy. Winnishiek, the Winnebago head chief, addressed the Ojibways, asking that they shake hands--"Brothers, the Great Spirit gave us hearts and skins alike, and will look down upon us when we shake hands." Hole-in-the-Day did not offer his hand, but ever the extremely intelligent analyst of political affairs, spoke on the subject of peace-making:

> **Ho! my brethren, we feel according to the purport of your conversation. We came here for that purpose. Although four distinct nations, we all speak and think alike. The subject we are talking about is the subject we meet to talk about. Now, I shall tell you how we met with our degradation. It was first by the Winnebagoes, second by the Sioux, third by the Chippewas, and fourth by the Americans.**
>
> **Brothers, it ought to be all our will in common--we must not forget the cause of our shame....Just look back twenty years ago. The treaty of peace you mentioned, was it ever kept? It was good for nothing--it was of no avail--it was never kept. It had no effect on the Indians whatever. It is a matter of great importance that we should come to a conclusion of our troubles. We all know our natures--how treacherous we are! We must mature a plan whereby our children may feel safe, and be safe when away from home.**
>
> **My friends, let us look back to our own way of making peace, and see whether it has ever been beneficial to us. It is a plain truth that we have looked upon you with smiling countenances ever since you have come in our country. There is a way in which our troubles can be settled, and we can look on each other with the same faces that we did before; and that way to bring satisfaction is to give us those that have committed the depredations on one another; and if we cannot come to any conclusions in this matter, we can never see the end of the depredations we may commit on each other....**

The Winnebagoes eventually gave up the guilty parties to a white sheriff. Still, the tribe was moved further south (to the Crow River), and in 1855 was removed to a new reserve on the Blue Earth River (south of Mankato, Minnesota).

Source: *Minnesota Democrat*, July 6, 1853.

BUFFALO

CHAPTER FIVE

FURTHER LAND SALE, 1855-1861

"...I am about to part with the graves of my fathers...."

"I do not hate the Sioux: I love them...."

HOLE-IN-THE-DAY February 14, 1855

HOLE-IN-THE-DAY made the first of his many trips to Washington in February 1855. He was accompanied by Crossing Sky, Bad Boy, Flat Mouth, and Buffalo, as well as Governor Gorman and trader Henry M. Rice. The chiefs had their first meeting with Indian Commissioner George Manypenny on February 14 in regard to selling their lands and taking reservations. During the discussions, Hole-in-the-Day took the opportunity to explain his views concerning inter-tribal relations, particularly with the Sioux. Paul H. Beaulieu interpreted on this occasion for the Ojibways (a job he would have off and on for the next thirty-five years).

> **My first study was how to make the long-sought for peace between the Chippewas and Sioux. I lost no opportunity to bring about that desirable result. The Chippewas have been assailed, their patience tried, and been persecuted, but, when attacked, have had revenge.**
>
> **My great study has been to secure peace, and, since I succeeded, have been trying to bring about peaceable and friendly relations with other tribes....**
>
> **With the Indians, as well as with the whites, there is an ambition to excel, and those who go to war generally delight in punishing their enemies. When I go, I do the same, and have revenge. [But] I do not hate the Sioux: I love them, as I do everyone on the continent who has a red skin. Of course, as I go to St. Paul very often, I frequently meet the Sioux and also the Winnebagoes. I shake hands with them, and, reminding them that the Indians once owned the continent, ask them where are they now. I tell them this everytime I see them, that, when they fight, they punish themselves and not the whites. I am a friend of peace.**

Everyone present, of course, knew well that Hole-in-the-Day had made repeated raids upon the Sioux; the commissioner said he was glad to hear these remarks made by the chief, and hoped that "a better day and destiny awaited the Chippewas."

Source: 1855 Treaty Negotiations with the Chippewas, February 14, 1855, typescript copy in James F. Sutherland Papers, MHS.

"...I am about to part with the graves of my fathers and to sell my birthright...."

FLAT MOUTH February 17, 1855

THE MISSISSIPPI OJIBWAY CHIEFS had been brought to Washington to cede over ten million acres of their land in northcentral Minnesota--more than half of it was prime timberland, covered with spruce, tamarack, and white pine. The government offered in return about a million and half dollars in payments, goods and services. The Pillager and Lake Winnibigoshish bands, however, would receive only an annual annuity of $10,666 for thirty years within the package. (Hole-in-the-Day initially commented that the Great Father was very "stingy.") In Flat Mouth's meeting with George Manypenny, he reflected on his age and his long history of friendship with the Americans. He went on to express his realization of the great consequences that the land cession would have for his people, and his wish for more money.

> **You see me here before you, father, and it would be useless for me to attempt to hide my age. My old head and gray hairs tell for themselves. I have seen a great many snows and rains. It is many years...since I first became acquainted with the Long Knives. A little before the war with Great Britain, I met them [the Pike expedition] ; they hugged and kissed me, and treated me with kindness, and promised to be my friend. Before that time I was a British subject. From this kind treatment of me may be dated my first connection with the Americans. Since then, my father, I have been their steady and fast friend....**
>
> **Do you see, my father? When I say a word, I stick to it. If my name is not recorded in the annals of history according to the whites, I feel that I am a big man with my tribe. They have witnessed my actions and know me....**
>
> **I call you father, a name which we as a people give to none among our tribe. We look up to you for protection. If I were traveling and met a person, and that person should be a spirit, I should ask that spirit for what I wanted. If I beg of you a little more money to clothe and provide for my children which I have left back, I hope you will excuse me. They are poor and in want, and expect me to protect their interests and provide for them....If I ask more than you offered, it is because I know you are rich, and I have left children behind me who are poor....**
>
> **Even if your heart was made of rock, father, if you would accompany me when I return to my home on the beautiful lake [Leech Lake] where I reside, and see my people coming nearly naked to meet me, and ascertain what their Great Father has done to relieve their wants, it would move your heart to pity.... You see...I am taking a great deal of pains to explain, because I am about to part with the graves of my fathers, and to sell my birthright....I am getting through...with my little speech. If you agree to its requests, when you see the Northern Lights running their way along the firmaments, after we reach our homes, they will convey to you the shouts and salutation of the Pillager band of Chippewas in gratitude for your kindness.**

Source: 1855 Treaty Negotiations, February 17, 1855, Sutherland Papers. Agent David Herriman said that Flat Mouth's speech 'took $120,000 [more ?] out of the national treasury.'(St. Anthony Falls) *Minnesota Republican*, April 12, 1855.

"We want to cease to be Indians and become Americans."

HOLE-IN-THE-DAY February 19, 1855

COMMISSIONER MANYPENNY'S basic offer of money to the Ojibways was $250,000. On February 19, 1855 Hole-in-the-Day said that the "offer was too small." He went on to explain that the Ojibways needed many things in order for them to begin cultivating the soil like the whites. He added, that if the commissioner drove such "a hard bargain" it would defeat his own view of civilizing the Indians. The chief then gave one of his best and most important speeches, pleading with the government to give them the means to become self-sufficient citizens:

> **I call upon the Master of Life to hear the words I am about to utter. I am about to talk respecting the property which I own. The Master of Life, who has made the world, has put us here. He has made everything we own for our benefit, that we may profit by it. Every man living may thank the Master of Life that he has placed him here, and given to him the means of making his support by his own exertions....**
>
> **Father, I am but poor and ignorant in my own estimation. I have not the power to express myself--I cannot overestimate myself. When I look all around me to the four corners of the earth, and at everything within my sight, and reflect upon what we are and have been, and what the whites are, I cannot but feel that a great weight of responsibility rests upon me in what I shall say and do on the present occasion.**
>
> **It is seven years ago since I first took my present position in my nation....It is seven years ago since I first began to exert myself for my people's advancement. In this, I have had the assistance of some annuities, and the assistance and advice of the whites.**
>
> **In thinking over the matter delegated to us, we have brought them, like mechanics, to perfection. We know the wants of the Chippewa nation--no one knows them better than ourselves, and we cannot be blamed if we look after and take care of our own best interests....We desire to convey to you our own ideas.**
>
> **My father, your name is the Long Knife. We call you father, because we look up to you for protection. Now, listen to what I shall say. You see us here--we the Chippewa Indians. We want you to be friendly. We do not want a mock show. Do not look upon us as you would upon the English. We are your children. We do not live outside, but within your nation. We are your friends. Why then look upon us as a foreign nation? My father, we want your friendship. No use of making of us a mock show as a separate nation. We want to give ourselves up to your government. We want to cease to be Indians, and become Americans. We want to be citizens, and to have the right to vote. All we desire is to imitate the whites, and to follow their example. We want to live as you do....A thick veil hides us from your view. Remove that veil, and see if we are not as good Americans as the whites....if you grant our request, and you should have a fight with any other nation, you can call upon us, and we will form a portion of your militia. We know how to fight, and will stand by you. We want the right of suffrage, the right to vote, to be subject to your laws, and have set our hearts upon it....**

Source: 1855 Treaty Negotiations, February 19, 1855, Sutherland Papers.

"Two great men have met!"

FLAT MOUTH March 9, 1855

FLAT MOUTH naively felt that he had been a hard bargainer in the treaty negotiations, having forced the Great Father to ask three times for the lands. On February 22 the treaty was signed, and on March 3 it was ratified by Congress. Six days later the chiefs were allowed to visit President Franklin Pierce at the executive mansion. Flat Mouth remarked:

> **Two great men have met....the whites were often accused of cheating the Indians, but this time the Indians had cheated the Commissioner, for they had sold him a tract of land for a good deal of money which was worth but little.**

President Pierce and Commissioner Manypenny laughed heartily, according to a newspaper reporter. And with good reason, for the land contained great timber stands, which alone were worth millions of dollars. Indeed, Flat Mouth and his fellow chiefs later regretted the deal, feeling that the government had broken many of its promises in regard to the treaty. The chief also complained that he had been bribed to sign it, but had not received the $2,000 bribe money.

Source: *Galena (IL) DailyAdvertiser*, March 20, 1855; Diedrich, *Chiefs Hole-in-the-Day*, 27; Flat Mouth's mention of a bribe, in *St. Paul Pioneer and Democrat*, Nov. 29, 1857.

"We did not know that such great treasures of copper were hidden in our land."

OJIBWAY SPEAKER **circa August 1855**

INDIAN COMMISSIONER GEORGE MANYPENNY attended the councils and annuity payments at LaPointe, on Madeline Island, in Lake Superior, in the late summer of 1855. He was addressed by a good number of Ojibway speakers, one of whom had been appointed by the chiefs to complain of American greediness for their lands and the nonfulfillment of treaty promises. A German traveler named Johann G. Kohl was present, and recorded the following speech:

> There is a Great Spirit from whom all good things here on earth come. He has given them to mankind--to the white as to the red men, for He sees no distinction of color. They must settle among themselves the possession of these things given by God.
>
> When the white men first came into this country and discovered us, we received them hospitably, and if they were hungry, we fed them, and went hunting for them. At first the white men only asked for furs and skins.... But for some years they have been asking land from us. For ten years they have asked from us nothing but land, and ever more land. We give unwillingly the land in which the graves of our fathers rest. But for all that, we have given land in our generosity. We knew not that we were giving so much for so little. We did not know that such great treasures of copper were hidden in our land.
>
> The white men have grown rich by the bargain. When I look around me in this assembly, I notice golden watch-chains and golden rings on the clothes and fingers of many men; and when I look in the faces of the people who are so richly adorned, I always see that their color is white, and not red. Among the red men I never see anything of the sort! ....We are not only poor, but we have also debts. On the former treaty and payment we also paid debts. I fancied then we paid them all. But now the old question is addressed to us. A number of old things are brought against us from an old bag. Where these debts come from, I know not--perhaps from the water!
>
> ....Our debts we will pay. But our land we will keep. As we have already given away so much, we will, at least, keep that land you have left us, and which is reserved for us....

Source: Johann G. Kohl, *Kitchi-Gami, Life Among the Lake Superior Ojibway* (St. Paul: Minnesota Historical Society Press, 1985), 53-57.

"Our suffering is always brought about by the folly of our chiefs."

HOLE-IN-THE-SKY circa August 1855

THIS OJIBWAY SPEAKER should not be confused with the elder or younger Hole-in-the-Days. Hole-in-the-Sky was (in 1855) a young man, about thirty years old, who lived among the Bad River Mission Ojibways, about fifteen miles from LaPointe. He addressed the council with Manypenny with great boldness, castigating the Ojibway chiefs for submitting to the influence of "other parties," and not the Indians. Observer Richard E. Morse mentioned that the speech was interpreted by Paul H. Beaulieu "of St. Paul, a half-breed, and a young man of fair English education, or rare gift of native talent, speaking with equal facility the English and the Indian...." Beaulieu had interpreted for the Mississippi Ojibways in Washington earlier that year.

My father, I stand here before you for the purpose of protecting the rights of our young men, women, and children. If I censure our chiefs, it is for the purpose of waking them up. Here, they are all before you; behold them now in your presence. Our suffering is always brought about by the folly of our chiefs. While they are negotiating, they are always influenced by other parties, and not by the Indians. They never consult the young men, although they are the owners of the soil, the same as the chiefs. The hard feeling existing between the young men and the chiefs is brought about by the chiefs never advising with the young men in regard to their actions....

My father, I came here to plead in behalf of our people. The chiefs do not think of us when they make bargains; they look to their own interests, but their people must take care of themselves the best they can. Is it possible we should see ourselves starve on account of our chiefs, and not open our mouths to speak?

Source: Richard E. Morse, "The Chippewas of Lake Superior," *Wisconsin Historical Collections* 3 (1857):350-51.

"...we drop to the ground like the trees before the axe of the white man...."

FEATHER'S END circa August 1855

FEATHER'S END, OR NAGUANABE, was the first chief of the Mille Lacs Ojibway bands in the early 1850s. He was a descendant of the hereditary chief of the Wolf totem--an interesting group of Ojibways who derived their origin on the paternal side from the Sioux.

At the annuity payment of 1855 at LaPointe, Feather's End was said to be "the smartest orator on the ground." He was about fifty-five years old, of medium height and weight; Richard Morse commented that the chief had "a very keen eye," which when animated in speaking, gave either "a sort of fiery look or a twinkle." The chief had his face painted with vermillion and wore an elaborate turban of turkey feathers over his head and shoulders. His speech was interpreted by Enmegahbowh, or John Johnson. He complained at length of promises unkept, saying that "perhaps it has sunk in the deep waters of the lake, or it may have evaporated in the heavens, like the rising mist--or perhaps it has blown over our heads, and gone towards the setting sun." He explained that he had difficulty getting trade goods from the traders and his agent, and had to live "principally in traveling through my home in the forest, by carrying the iron [gun] on my shoulder...." He went on to say:

> **My father, look around you upon the faces of my poor people; sickness and hunger, whiskey and war are killing us fast. We are dying and fading away; we drop to the ground like the trees before the axe of the white man; we are weak--you are strong. We are but foolish Indians--you have knowledge and wisdom in your head; we want your help and protection. We have no homes--no cattle--no lands, and we will not long need them. A few short winters and my people will be no more. The winds shall soon moan around the last lodge of your red children. I grieve, but cannot turn our fate away. The sun--the moon--the rivers--the forest, we love so well, we must leave. We shall soon sleep in the ground--we will not awake again. I have no more to say to you, my father.**

At some point during the proceedings, an agent asked the chief if he had understood the articles of the treaty he had signed in 1854. Feather's End replied:

> **My father, I was there last year when the treaty was made, and I swallowed the words of the treaty down my throat, and they have not yet had time to blister my breast.**

Sources: Morse, "Chippewas of Lake Superior," 340-44; *Henderson Democrat*, July 24, 1856. Trader Henry M. Rice described Feather's End in 1849 as "a sober Indian," but a "great gabber." He said that the chief was not a hereditary chief and was not generally consulted by the "real chiefs." Henry Rice to Jonathan Fletcher, May 17, 1849, Office of Indian Affairs, Winnebago Agency, Letters Received, microfilm copy in MHS.

"I can see nothing, as nothing is to be seen."

FLAT MOUTH August 26, 1858

FLAT MOUTH was extremely disappointed with the results of the Treaty of 1855. On several occasions in the late 1850s he complained bitterly "of the neglect of their Great Father in Washington to fufill treaty obligations." He had hoped to see schools built, farming implements provided, and land broken for cultivation, but even two or three years later nothing had been done. In August 1858 he was visited by the new Ojibway agent, James Lynde; Paul Beaulieu and Charles Charlo served as interpreters. Also among the visitors was Charles E. Flandrau, a one-year Sioux agent in 1856-57. He wrote down the following speech of Flat Mouth.

> I thank the Great Spirit that our present agent was present at that treaty [of 1855] as he knows what promises were made and can see for himself how they have been fulfilled. I only went when I heard the voice of the Great Father for the third time for the good of my people and not to be a great chief, as that I have from my blood.
>
> I can see nothing as nothing is to be seen. We wrote a letter to our Great Father telling our complaints, but have never heard from it. When that treaty was written I thought it was for the good of my people. You have explained it, and we understand it, but it has not been fulfilled, and we bow our heads and are quiet. The money is absorbed in claims. Our schoolmasters have clothed themselves out of our money and our white chiefs say they will remedy it, but as yet we see nothing but promises--no remedy....
>
> It is with great anxiety that we look for the first goods that you are to distribute among us and whether they will go round. We do not think our Great Father would cheat us, although he asked three times for our land before we sold it. I do not want to be understood that I blame the Great Father only for the delay.
>
> I look back over my life and see a straight road. I know that all the evils we suffer are from liquor, and I will aid you to keep it out as long as this lake bears its name. We can see the effects of liquor among our brethren of the Mississippi. I cannot help loving it, although I know its baneful effect. I see the once strong chiefs of my people looking like trees in winter without a leaf to cover them, but still I love the influence of it.

Buffalo, Big Dog's Son, and Majigabo also made speeches. Buffalo asked Lynde to "let nothing tempt him to wrong them," intimating that some agents had; he also said that he was ashamed that he had helped sell his lands for an annuity which gave him only a shirt and one pair of leggings!

Sources: Flandrau Journal, August 26, 1858, Charles E. Flandrau Papers, MHS; *St. Paul Pioneer and Democrat*, Nov. 29, 1857. A reporter in 1857 commented of Flat Mouth--that when he was in the prime of life "he was looked upon as the finest orator among all the Indians," and that even now "at his advanced age, when he warms with his subject, he exerts a powerful influence over his auditors."

"Me never more will drink whiskey."

MANITOWAB July 25, 1859

THE WHISKEY TRADE to the Mississippi Ojibways flourished in the late 1850s. The town of Crow Wing, in fact, was composed almost entirely of saloons! As Claude Beaulieu (a descendant of the famous mixed-blood Crow Wing trader, Clement Beaulieu) said--they did not sell it at the counter, but "at the back door by bottle, jug, and even five gallon keg...." At annuity payments, many of the Indians would take their cash and spend it on liquor.

In the summer of 1859 the Ojibway bands of Gull Lake were in particularly bad straits: hot weather had killed many of the fish and berries upon which they depended for subsistence in the summer, and what assets the Ojibways did have, were often spent on whiskey. One of the Gull Lake bands composed of about one hundred Christian Indians decided to send their chief, Manitowab, to St. Cloud, to ask the white people for assistance. He made his address on July 25, 1859, either in his own broken English, or that of the interpreter's.

> **Me have to say a few words. Me came down and see you and see all white men in your country. They good Indian, live up at Gull Lake. They send me down to see you and your towns. They told me to come down and see you. They have nothing to eat, nothing to wear. Me never more will drink whiskey....We will tell all the Indians to give up...whiskey, dress like all the white people dress....**

Sources: On Crow Wing, see Claude Beaulieu article in *Brainerd Dispatch*, April 19, 1918; *St. Cloud Democrat*, July 28, 1859. Manitowab is variously translated as "Sees Like God" and "Supernatural Vision."

"Our shadows rest on our graves."

FLAT MOUTH Fall 1859

FLAT MOUTH was about eighty-five years old in 1859, and soon to die. He had become rather embittered about Chippewa-white relations, especially after making the Treaty of 1855. When he heard, in the fall of 1859, that the government was cutting down pine trees on his reservation--without his knowledge, he determined to retaliate: he sent his young men to kill cattle and take goods belonging to the government. Shortly afterwards, the new Episcopal bishop of Minnesota, Henry B. Whipple, arrived at Leech Lake, and offered to help settle the difficulty. In a council with the bishop, the old chief vented his frustrations in a speech of which Whipple recorded the following few lines:

> **I suppose you came to find out who killed the government cattle. I did! You want to know who took the government goods [?]. I did! I told my young men to do it. Perhaps you want to know why we did it. We have been robbed. We have been robbed again and again. We will bear it no longer. Our shadows rest on our graves.**

Whipple said that the chief continued at great length, angry, exasperated, and using bitter invective and stinging sarcasm. Whipple, however, reasoned with the chief, saying "When I ask good [white] men to help me, and they ask if the Indians for whom I am pleading are the ones who killed those cattle and stole those goods, what shall I say?" Flat Mouth apologized, and Whipple succeeded in halting the cutting of Indian pine. The chief later gave Whipple a beautiful stole made of black beads, with a gold cross on each end.

The chief died apparently during the winter of 1859-60. Francis Pierz, a Catholic missionary, wrote in 1860: "In Leech Lake I heard to my sorrow that the grand chief, Eskibakaj, who was recognized as king of the entire Ojibway nation, had died from stomach cramp in the past winter." Pierz states that the chief had sent for him that he might be baptized; but Pierz was unable to make it. The chief's epitaph could have been his words to Governor Henry Dodge in 1837: "Wherever I have been the print of the white men's hands have been left upon my own....My ancestors were chiefs of the tribes and villages while they lived. I do not, however, hold my title from them, but have obtained it by my own acts and merits." The chief's son, Leading Bird of Prey (Niganibines), better known as Flat Mouth II, later became a prominent leader among the Ojibway.

Sources: Henry B. Whipple, "Civilization and Christianization of the Ojibways in Minnesota," *Minnesota Historical Collections* 9 (1901):138-39; Francis Pierz to Leopold Foundation, Jan. 18, 1860, in Manuscripts Relating to Northwest Missions, Nute Papers; "Proceedings of Council with the Chippewa Indians," 417.

"I shall plant a tree where you preached today...."

WADENA, BAD BOY, and WHITE FISHER — July 1860 and February 1861

IN THE FALL OF 1859 Henry B. Whipple was appointed the Episcopal bishop of Minnesota. Within two weeks of his arrival in the state, he traveled north to visit the St. Columba Mission among the Ojibways at Gull Lake, which had been established seven years before by James Lloyd Breck. The following summer, Whipple began to carry his message of advocating "civilized life" and Christianity to other Chippewa villages. He preached at White Fish Lake on July 22, 1860, and was listened to by Wadena, who had been a headman among the Gull Lakers, and who was a cousin and brother-in-law of Chief Bad Boy. Wadena afterwards told Whipple:

> **My father's words are true, but he does know that they are dark to me. He can easy[ly] say it is better to be civilized and to be [a] Christian. See my people. We have no oxen, no tools, no horses--nothing to do as the white man does. We have no seeds, no schools. We know the Grand Medicine, but we do not know your religion. We are in the dark and need the light, and our white friends must be patient.**
>
> **I came here from Gull Lake, because I wanted to get away from the firewater. I desired to avoid it for we all fall into its temptation. My fathers used to live here. I shall plant a tree where you have preached today, and when my children grow up that tree will tell where the first white missionary stood that preached on the banks of White Fish Lake.**

On a return visit to Ojibway country in February 1861, Whipple held a council with the Gull Lake chiefs, pleading for them to abstain from "fire water--which now flows like [a] river of death thro[ugh] all the borders." Bad Boy was among those who responded. He was born in about 1805 at Elbow Lake (Cass County), but raised at Gull Lake. After his half-brother, Little Curly Head, was killed by the Sioux, he became a chief. He had welcomed the Breck Mission in 1852 and had always spoken favorably of the need for the Ojibways to become Christians, and particularly to abstain from whiskey:

> **My father's words are very heavy. They are heavy because they are true. They are the best counsel we ever had. I am hoarse and sick because I have been using the fire water. I have often quit, and then commenced its use again....We must obey our father's words if we want to live. I speak not because I am the head man, but for my people. It does my heart good to hear your words. I wish I had the power to act for my people, then I would stop its use at once. I have not long to live, but we must act for our children....If we had all obeyed when the missionary came ten years ago, we should have been a happier people. I know the fire water keeps us from the Great Spirit....**

Old White Fisher (who had formerly companied with the Elder Chief Hole-in-the-Day) added that the whiskey had made him "old, sick, and poor." He entreated Whipple: "My father, you are [the] head man to speak to the Great Spirit. He will hear you when you speak. Will you not speak for your Red children, and ask that they may be saved from the fire water[?] I have done."

Source: Henry B. Whipple diaries, July 22, 1860, Feb. 4, 1861, in Protestant Episcopal Church Papers, MHS.

"It is time for us to ask some compensation...."

RED BEAR August 30, 1861

RED BEAR and his brother, Little Chief, were the leaders of the Pembina Ojibway. They had watched with much concern as the whites, particularly J. C. Burbank and Company, began to navigate the waters of the Red River with the steamboat "Pioneer." Not only did the steamer scare away game, but the whites also helped themselves to timber along the way for fuel. On August 30, 1861 Red Bear, Right in the Middle, and He Who is Spoken To (the young Red Lake chief), met in council with Alden Bryant, the captain of the steamboat, and other officials of Pembina. Red Bear made the following speech:

> My brother Little Chief, having invested me with authority to act for him, considering what shall be done by me as done by himself, says that the steamboat Pioneer is navigating the waters of the Red River.
>
> We are poor and have never received anything for it. We have been raised here and have always resided in this place. The bones of my father lie buried on the point of Pembina. We want the boat to give us something whenever she shall pass. We have never disturbed the boat, but the time has arrived when she should give us something.
>
> We ask a compensation for our wood. If not paid [to] us, we will make known our complaints to the Governor [Alexander Ramsey]. If we do not receive any satisfaction from the boat, then the boat shall be stopped....We want one thousand dollars in money, or one keg of money as sent by the Governor to Indian payments. It is time for us to ask for some compensation for our wood and the use of the river.
>
> Let them not take us for fools. We know what we are doing. We want five chests of tea, three barrels of sugar, one keg of powder, two sacks of shot, one sack of balls, two sacks of flour, one box of tobacco, some guns and ammunition to defend ourselves against the Sioux, who are reported to be coming to attack us. If we are granted what we ask, we shall get along, otherwise we do not know what will become of us....

He Who is Spoken To added: "We don't hate your boat, but you are doing us a great injury. You are driving our game all away. It is not for ourselves that we speak, but for our children, and we find it very hard since the boat began to run. Our hunting grounds have all been given up...." Captain Bryant yielded to the demands of the chiefs and gave out some goods. The chiefs wished to see Burbank about the matter at Georgetown in October. When they arrived they found that no arrangements had been made to make a settlement; the Red Lakers vented their frustration by shooting a pig and robbing a house. When Burbank heard the news he asked Governor Ramsey to send troops to Georgetown and to have him write to the Red Lake chief to threaten him with "the strong arm of their Great Father."

Sources: Account of Council at Pembina, August 30, 1861, Alex Murray to J. C. Burbank, Oct. 23, 1861, J. C. Burbank to Gov. Ramsey, Nov. 7, 1861, in Governors' Records, MHS.

HOLE-IN-THE-DAY II

CHAPTER SIX

HOLE-IN-THE-DAY'S REVOLT; 1862-1863

"...they had been promised redress, but it had never come...."

"...he believes the present agent...is not acting justly with his tribe."

HOLE-IN-THE-DAY June 11, 1862

IN THE SPRING OF 1861, Republican territorial legislator Lucius C. Walker was appointed the Mississippi Ojibway agent, replacing James Lynde. In early December, Walker and superintendent Clark W. Thompson made the annuity payment at Crow Wing. Hole-in-the-Day was quite sure that money had been withheld from them, and trader Clement Beaulieu discovered that Walker had altered the payroll lists to cover up a steal of about $8,000. Hole-in-the-Day decided to go to Washington to see commissioner William P. Dole about the matter; he arrived at the capitol in early June 1862, along with trader George Morrison and interpreter Peter Roy. They helped the chief with the interpretation and writing of a letter to Dole on June 11, in which he stated his accusations against Walker:

> **At the annual payment last fall, his Indians did not receive the usual amount of money. He has not been able[to find out why], and desires to know the reason. And he wishes the Commissioner will allow him to see and examine the pay roll of last fall's payment, which the agent, Major Walker, sent to Washington.**
>
> **....He wishes to say that he believes the present agent, Maj. Walker, is not acting justly with his tribe, and that his removal is desired by himself and all the Indians he represents. But as the department may be unwilling to act on his mere opinion, he respectfully suggests that the Commissioner either send a reliable person from Washington, or appoint a reliable person in Minnesota or elsewhere, to go to Crow Wing and investigate the condition of affairs and particularly the manner in which Major Walker has discharged his trust....**

Dole allowed Hole-in-the-Day to examine the payroll. He found that Beaulieu had been right. The chief, for example, saw that the roll listed him as having received $600, when he had only gotten $300. He further requested of Dole to "call upon Major Walker for such explanations as he may be able to give, and trusting that the wrongs practised or attempted upon his band may be corrected with a firm and unsparing hand."

Source: Mark Diedrich, "Chief Hole-in-the-Day and the 1862 Chippewa Disturbance: A Reappraisal," *Minnesota History* (Spring 1987), 50:197-200. According to William S. King, a Republican associate of Cyrus Aldrich and Clark Thompson (the superintendent of Indian affairs in Minnesota), Commissioner Dole "furnished 'Hole' with necessary papers to prefer charges against Walker and he [Walker] will have to be brought before you [Thompson] to answer to the indictment." King to Clark W. Thompson, June 27, 1862, Thompson Papers, MHS.

"We shall look foolish when we are hanged."

BUFFALO circa August 20, 1862

HOLE-IN-THE-DAY returned from Washington in late June 1862, expecting that commissioner William P. Dole would take action in removing agent Walker from office and investigating his apparent fraud. Nothing happened, and by mid-August, the chief was furious over the lack of response. Then he learned that the whites were recruiting Ojibway mixedbloods for service in the Union Army. He decided to use this as an issue to stir up a hostile demonstration against the whites in order to get attention to his complaints against Walker. Word was sent to Leech Lake that the "Great Father intended to send men and take all the Indians and dress them like soldiers, and send them away to fight in the south, and if we wished to save ourselves we must rise and fight the whites...." The Ojibways killed several head of cattle at the agency. In response to this depredation, Walker, on August 19, ordered soldiers from Fort Ripley to arrest Hole-in-the-Day. The chief, however, eluded capture and sent another message to Leech Lake, telling the Pillagers to exterminate the whites there, that soon there wouldn't be a white man left at Crow Wing. The Leech Lake chiefs Big Dog and Buffalo resisted Hole-in-the-Day's message to kill the whites, though several were taken prisoner and their goods taken. Buffalo reasoned with his warriors in this way:

> **I am older than you. We have received a message to kill the white men. White men have wronged us and perhaps they ought to die. Hole-in-the-Day says there is war, that the Indians will drive the white men out of the country, that these men must be killed. If we go to the white men's settlements and find that there is no war, we shall be asked by the Great Father what has become of his white children. We shall look foolish when we are hanged. We can kill these men as well next week as today.**

The Pillagers spared the lives of their prisoners and then went down to Gull Lake to join up with the Ojibways there under Hole-in-the-Day. Buffalo's suspicions were correct--no whites had been killed, though a war scare had begun. By an unusual coincidence, the Sioux had commenced a war on the whites of the Minnesota River valley at precisely the same time that Hole-in-the-Day had begun his demonstrations!

Sources: Diedrich, *Chiefs Hole-in-the-Day*, 33-34; Henry B. Whipple, *Lights and Shadows of a Long Episcopate* (New York: Macmillan Co.,1899), 317. Buffalo died on January 7, 1868, at about the age of seventy-five. He was considered as "a friend of the whites." *Minneapolis Daily Times*, Jan. 26, 1868.

"...if you are the smartest man the Great Father has got, I pity our Great Father."

HOLE-IN-THE-DAY September 10, 1862

WITH ALARMS CIRCULATING northern Minnesota that the Ojibways were preparing for war, William P. Dole, the commissioner of Indian affairs, left off his journey to meet the Red Lake Ojibways, to meet with Hole-in-the-Day at Fort Ripley. However, the chief refused to place his security in jeapordy, and agreed only to meet Dole at Crow Wing. The Commissioner was chagrined to see the chief at the head of three hundred men--some of whom quickly circuited the whites and cut them off from the road behind. Dole told the chief that he would be glad to hear their grievances. Hole-in-the-Day shook hands with all of the notables present, but then replied very bluntly:

> **Are you the smartest man that our Great Father could send in a trying time like this? Because, if you are the smartest man the Great Father has got, I pity our Great Father. You have been talking to me as if I was a child. I am not a little child. I have gray hairs on my head. I may not be as smart as you are, but your talk sounds to me like babytalk....You say the treaty reads so and so. Now that is a lie and you know it.**

Trader Daniel Mooers commented that the chief took Dole's speech "from beginning to end, word for word, and when he got through it was like a stocking that has been unraveled--there was nothing left of it." The council was broken off, Hole-in-the-Day leaving unmolested, despite the presence of one hundred soldiers under Captain Francis Hall. Dole reported to Governor Ramsey--"In the council Hole-in-the-Day was bold and impudent, and no result was reached by the conference."

Sources: Diedrich, *Chiefs Hole-in-the-Day*, 35; William P. Dole to Gov. Ramsey, Sept. 11, 1862, in Governors' Records.

"...Hole-in-the-Day stole the senses of our young men and led them to do bad deeds...."

BUFFALO September 13, 1862

AFTER THE FRUITLESS COUNCIL with Commissioner Dole, Hole-in-the-Day continued to remain hostile to the whites. Dole left for St. Paul and appointed Ashley C. Morrill as special agent to resolve the difficulties. Morrill visited the Indian camp and was successful in disintegrating the weakened resolve of the Pillager chiefs to stand with Hole-in-the-Day. The following day, September 13, Buffalo, Majigabo, Young Man's Son, and others surrendered to Morrill. Buffalo spoke of the many injustices to his tribe which helped precipitate their "bad acts":

> My father, my heart is glad to meet you today in council and to be able to tell you that we are sorry for our bad acts; yet we are not wholly to blame; we, too, have some complaints to lay before you that we want you to tell to our Great Father at Washington.
>
> Nearly eight years ago, when we were leaving Washington [1855], we were promised by our Great Father ten boxes of money, and we were told at the same time that the following spring, at sugar making, we should have a present of goods to the like amount. These promises thus made to us were not kept; we never saw this money or these goods; here we claim twenty boxes ($20,000). Then we were to have four thousand dollars a year to dispose of at pleasure; if a young man wanted a gun or a coat we could buy it out of this money...but we have never seen this money; here we claim thirty boxes. We were to have blacksmiths among us and iron furnished to do our work; true, we have seen the blacksmith, but he is always out of iron....Here again we claim a loss; then our goods are not sufficient to clothe us, and we were promised at Washington that our women and children should be kept warm by the goods sent to them by their Great Father; here is another claim, maybe six boxes. We were promised carpenters to build houses for our old men and for the chiefs; we have not seen the carpenters; here again we have lost....Then our school; true, we have them, but our children are not clothed as we wish, and though our children go to school, they are not made wise; perhaps they are to blame....
>
> I think, since our treaty, that there is sixty boxes due us from our Great Father. But I do not blame him; we think that he sends us what is due us; perhaps our annuities are lost at St. Paul; perhaps here at Crow Wing; perhaps at the agency, or, as the road from Washington is long and crooked, and the fore car moves so very fast, perhaps they drop off and are lost over the road.

The young men present then wanted the chiefs to say who it was that advised them to make the outbreak. Following Majigabo and Wesac, Buffalo said:

> You ask who was the cause of this. It was Hole-in-the-Day. He whispered evil things in the ears of our young men and they refused to listen to us. We have always been friends to the whites; by them we live....When would we see our payment again if we fought the whites? But Hole-in-the-Day stole the senses of our young men and led them to do bad deeds to the whites.

Source: 37 Congress, 3 session, *House Executive Document*, vol. 2, 1862-63 (serial 1157), 219-20.

"...I would have nothing to do with it."

BAD BOY September 1862

BAD BOY was the second chief of the Gull Lake Ojibway, having ninety-four people in his band. He knew, as did Hole-in-the-Day, that something was amiss when Agent Walker made the Ojibway payment the previous fall. He received $20.00 in surplus money and later learned that Walker had put him down for $150.00 on the payroll. Still, the chief flatly refused to join Hole-in-the-Day in his revolt. When trouble started, Bad Boy fled Gull Lake and joined the whites at Fort Ripley. He later gave testimony regarding Hole-in-the-Day, apparently to special agent Ashley Morrill, with probable interpretation by John Johnson Enmegahbowh. His statements give credence to the popular theory that Hole-in-the-Day and the Dakota chief Little Crow were involved in a conspiracy together to fight the whites:

> A year ago last summer [1861], Hole-in-the-Day's headman came to me and told me that Hole-in-the-Day was about to make a treaty with the Sioux, and that they were to fight the whites together. I said to him to tell Hole-in-the-Day it was a very wrong step if he intends to do what you say. Afterwards, the Mille Lac chiefs came to me and wanted to know what Hole-in-the-Day was doing. I told them the whole story. They all said it was a very bad business and we will have nothing to do with it, and that is the reason I think why they were not seen at Gull Lake.
>
> Afterward, I met Hole-in-the-Day and had a talk with him. He said, "I wanted to see you some time ago. I want your assistance in my undertaking." I told him I know all about it, for your head man had told me and I would have nothing to do with it....
>
> Hole-in-the-Day's head man told me that Hole-in-the-Day had sent six men to rob and murder Mr. Cloeter [the Lutheran missionary at Rabbit Lake] and family. He told me also we were going to kill all the Indians that join the whites....He also told me they were going to attack the fort and then to fall back to the British Possessions, and then get the Indians up there to help us.

Source: Special File 201, Office of Indian Affairs, microfilm copy in MHS.

"...they had been promised redress, but it had never come...."

HOLE-IN-THE-DAY September 15, 1862

AFTER COMMISSIONER DOLE left Crow Wing, Hole-in-the-Day planned to make a show of force against the agency (which was guarded by soldiers), but the Pillager chiefs decided to have nothing more to do with the "uprising." On September 13 they surrendered to special agent Ashley C. Morrill, leaving Hole-in-the-Day no choice but to do the same. However, due to Dole's failure, the Minnesota state legislature sent the so-called "St. Paul Commissioners" to Crow Wing to settle the affair. The members of the commission were Henry M. Rice, Judge David Cooper, Edwin A. C. Hatch, and missionary Frederick Ayer; Governor Ramsey was also present. During a council on September 15, Hole-in-the-Day was quoted in substance as saying:

> **That they had sold their land to the government; that they had been promised a great many things in return, but had never received them; that they had complained to their Great Father of these things, and had been promised redress [by Dole], but it had never come; that they were now poor and in rags, as we could see, the whole wealth of their bands being upon the backs of those present, and their families at home naked; but if they had been fairly dealt with, they would not now be in that miserable condition.**

The chief requested that someone should come and investigate their affairs, in whose selection they might have a voice, that all things should be looked into, including "the charges made against the Indians, as well as those made by them." Commissioner Dole had undoubtedly failed to make an investigation of Walker, as the chief had requested earlier that summer, in order to coverup the frauds perpetrated by the agent, as well as those higher up, particularly Superintendent Clark Thompson, and the Republican congressmen who helped place him in that office. St. Paul lawyer John M. Gilman implied this when he wrote to Thompson that "Ramsey...will claim the gratitude of the country for repairing the mischief which the Genl [Dole], yourself, Maj. Walker, & Col. [Cyrus] Aldrich have done." A treaty was drawn up in which it was agreed that there would be peace between the Chippewas and the government, charges would be investigated, and annuities would be paid intact within thirty days. Although the state government had no real authority to make such an agreement, the federal government honored the stipulations. Still, no real investigation was made into Walker's conduct. Instead Thompson wrote reports which shifted all the blame for the revolt on Hole-in-the-Day.

Source: Diedrich, "Chief Hole-in-the-Day and the 1862 Chippewa Disturbance," 193-203. J. C. Hicks of Sauk Rapids wrote to Governor Ramsey: "We feel that the Indians have been outraged by dishonest men in high places in the government....The [Cyrus] Aldrich faction would in a moment sacrifice the peace, happiness, and prosperity of this whole country to prevent an investigation into the horrid crimes and iniquities that have been perpetrated upon the poor Indian and for that reason....were we glad to see you here, hoping that your advent would be the commencement of a rigid investigation." Hicks to Ramsey, Sept. 4, 1862, Ramsey Papers, MHS.

"The cause of our removal is the mischief Hole-in-the-Day's party have done."

SHABASHKUNG and SON of BEAR'S HEART January 19, 1863

DUE TO THE CHIPPEWA DISTURBANCE, President Abraham Lincoln sent the assistant secretary of the interior, John P. Usher, to Minnesota to help restore the peace. In late November 1862 Usher met with Hole-in-the-Day, and a plan was agreed upon whereby the Mississippi Ojibway would give up their Gull Lake reserve for one in the vicinity of Leech Lake. However, John Johnson, who had no love for the chief, felt that Hole-in-the-Day was only using the new treaty arrangement so as to be "in a condition to steal larger sums of money from his people...." On January 19, 1863 a number of chiefs, including Shabashkung of Mille Lacs, and Bad Boy of Gull Lake, met with Bishop Whipple at Crow Wing. Shabashkung, who had been appointed as speaker for the chiefs, said:

> When I was a young boy about six years old, I heard the old men of our people say that in the course of time we would be removed. I have had many thoughts about it and now the evil has come and all for the conduct of one bad man.
>
> Your hands are clean, and I am not worthy to speak to you. I am very small and I have no right to come to you, but I, and my people, are in trouble and want your advice. We have plenty of land at Mille Lac, more than we can use. When we went to Washington it was given for our homes and now we are to be removed for one bad man. The reason why I tell you this is that I am very small and have no one to assist us and we are fading away. There are many chiefs older than I am, and though younger, they ask me to speak.
>
> We held a council at the time of the outbreak and all agreed to keep from wronging the whites. I said to all our young men to keep away from the outbreak. I advised them to be friends and said if they go they can never come back here. I wish to live, friends, to till the ground and have my children taught, for it's our only hope....
>
> Your clothing is that of a white man, but there is room in your heart for the red man too. I have found out that the way we are living is not the way to please the Great Spirit. Now we have concluded to throw away our blankets if our Great Father will help us.
>
> We have thought a great deal about the wrongs of the red man, and we have more right to ask you to assist us than the bad Indians, who have done this wrong. While I was sitting in my wigwam, I heard this bad news that we are to be removed. There is such war in my mind I cannot sleep nights....I will say no more--tell me plainly as a brother what the whites think.

The son of Bear's Heart then added:

> The cause of our removal is the mischief Hole-in-the-Day's party have done....It is only one man who always troubles us and we will never move with him again. The man is Hole-in-the-Day. He is the man who ought to be removed. He has spilt white man's blood and will spill it again and ought to be punished.

Source: Henry B. Whipple Diary, Jan. 19, 1863, Protestant Episcopal Church Papers, MHS.

"Has not your Great Father given you everything you asked him for?"

SITS AHEAD circa January 1863

DUE TO THE OJIBWAY INDIAN TROUBLES, the government allowed agent Luther E. Webb of the Lake Superior Ojibways to bring a delegation to Washington. The chiefs on the trip included Little Pine (La Pointe), Little Bee (Lac du Flambeau), He Sews (Lac Court Oreilles), Cut Ear (Bad River), and Sits Ahead, or Naganub (Fond du Lac).

Sits Ahead had become the leading chief at Fond du Lac after the deaths of Loon's Foot and Spruce. He was about forty-eight in 1863, short and close built, a dandy in dress, polite, and neat in attire. Of his oratory, Richard Morse wrote in 1855: "He is very intelligent, for a man of the woods. None surpassed him as an impressive orator; his language is rapid and vehement--his gestures quick and flashy; his whole action and look, when excited in speech, is so wild that they similate the maniac. His audience was usually well impressed with his words; he frequently indulged in irony....he is full of the fire of eloquence; he is the beau ideal of an Indian chief."

The delegation, upon leaving Lake Superior, went to St. Paul and then to Chicago, where they visited Camp Douglas. Here they saw a number of Confederate soldiers, who were being held as prisoners of war. With Benjamin Armstrong interpreting, Sits Ahead addressed the crowd:

> **You have been fighting against our government. Why do you do this? Has not your Great Father given you everything you asked him for? He gives to the palefaces and the Indians plenty to eat and good clothes to wear. He makes good laws for the best government of all. He makes the laws for the many --for all his people, not to suit a few.**
>
> **You have been fighting to break up this government, like the bloody Sioux. It is better that you stop fighting and lay down your arms, and come back and be brothers again. If you will think with your holiest thoughts about your country, you will know you are wrong. If you feel as if you must fight against them, look at your clothes and then look at ours. Our Great Father feeds and clothes us.**

The chief's great faith in the government, so strong at this time, later diminished greatly. About twenty years later he wrote a long and detailed letter to Minnesota governor Lucius Hubbard, recounting numerous instances in which he felt that the government had not fulfilled promises and failed to act honorably in many treaty situations.

Sources: Morse, "Chippewas of Lake Superior," 346-49; *St. Paul Daily Press*, Feb. 1, 1863; *The Progress* (White Earth Agency), Feb. 18, 1888. Sits Ahead sent a letter to Gov. Alexander Ramsey, offering to fight the Sioux if the government would pay the expense in the fall of 1862. *Mankato Record*, Sept. 12, 1862.

SITS AHEAD

"...we have in a great measure forgot nature's teachings in the virtue of roots, herbs, and plants."

SITS AHEAD **March 1863**

AFTER A VISIT with President Abraham Lincoln in Washington, the Lake Superior chiefs were brought on a visit to New York. Here they met the medicine man and chief of the Mic-Mac tribe of Nova Scotia. He spoke to them of a medicine he had prepared for the cure of smallpox, and gave the Ojibways a sample. Sits Ahead made the following eloquent response:

> Surely, my brethren, it is the will of the Great Spirit that has conducted us here to meet with our brother who is present, and surely the medicine that he has discovered is invaluable; it will be a benefit to the whole world. The disease which it is intended to cure has taken away a multitude of our own people, which, had we been in possession of such an invaluable remedy, we still would be a great nation.
>
> Brother, we thank you and your people. We, as a great nation, were the original owners of this great country; our forefathers inhabited this country. Nature taught them that out of the bosom of the earth, they should dig the root and pluck the herb and the plant for medicinal purposes. We have been reduced into small bands by the disease; the white man has crowded us out of our country, by which we have in a great measure forgot nature's teachings in the virtue of roots, herbs, and plants. Therefore, it is gratifying to know that your people still retain some reminiscence of the knowledge of roots, herbs, and plants, which nature taught our forefathers how to prepare. Brother, we accept this present from your hands with grateful hearts, and again I repeat, we thank you and your people.

Source: *St. Paul Daily Press*, March 21, 1863. Sits Ahead made trips to Washington in 1852, 1863, and again in 1866. *St. Paul Pioneer*, Feb. 11, 1866.

SHABASHKUNG

CHAPTER SEVEN

STRUGGLE FOR A FUTURE, 1863-1868

"I see salvation for my children in that place--White Earth...."

"...my people learned that the chiefs who had gone to Washington had exchanged their homes for a mere swamp and marsh...."

HOLE-IN-THE-DAY June 7, 1863

AFTER THE AFFAIR at Crow Wing had been settled in late 1862, a number of the Mississippi chiefs were brought by Henry M. Rice to Washington to make a new treaty--Hole-in-the-Day was conspicuous in his absence. By a treaty signed on March 11, 1863, all of the reservations for the Mississippi bands established by the Treaty of 1855 were ceded for a reserve near Leech Lake. When the chiefs returned there was great opposition to what they had done. At Rabbit Lake a fight broke out during which a chief and two headmen were killed--it was reported that chiefs who had no hand in the treaty vowed to kill those who signed it! On June 7, 1863 Hole-in-the-Day dictated a letter to be sent to President Lincoln. He said that the new reserve would bring the bands closer to the whiskey trade from Lake Superior, and that the land was mostly unfit for agriculture. He warned that the young men were discontented, and that further troubles might occur if nothing was done to rectify the situation. He continued:

> **When the news of the treaty reached us at the agency, I did everything to make them satisfied, without knowing what the provisions of the treaty were; but when my people learned that the chiefs who had gone to Washington had exchanged their homes for a mere swamp and marsh, and had received and given away, or idly spent, so large a sum as sixteen thousand dollars of their arrearage fund, it was impossible to restore quiet, and equally impossible to preserve the peace. Occasionally they would seem contented, but the moment they got whiskey among them, the opposition to the treaty would manifest itself, and three of my people, one head chief, and two subordinate ones, were killed....**
>
> **Give us some assurance, my father, that you sometimes think of us, and when you do, that it is of our welfare, that you have our interest at heart, and that we may live in hope that new and proper homes will be given us.... I speak this in behalf of and in the name of my people, and beseech you, my father, to open your ears and heart to what I have said....**

Sources: *St. Paul Pioneer*, May 8, 1863; Diedrich, *Chiefs Hole-in-the-Day*, 39-40; 38 Congress, 1 Session, *House Document*, Vol. 3, 1863-64, 447-51. The chief proposed that he be allowed to make a new treaty for a reserve on the Wild Rice River--an area which later became a part of the White Earth Reservation.

"...we want nothing to do with you or with your plans."

LITTLE BOY September 22, 1863

INDIAN COMMISSIONER William P. Dole came to Minnesota in August 1862, intending to make a treaty with the Red Lake and Pembina Ojibway bands; but the plans were frustrated by the outbreak of war with the Sioux, as well as the threat of trouble with Hole-in-the-Day and his warriors near Crow Wing. However, in September 1863 the government made another attempt to treat with the Red Lakers, this time with Governor Ramsey and special agent Ashley Morrill acting as commissioners. The treaty was designed to pacify the bands of that region (who had been disturbed by steamboat runs on the Red River), and to gain land on which a railroad might traverse, opening the way for commercial intercourse between Canada and the United States.

The Red Lakers were surprised when Chief Hole-in-the-Day arrived to attend the treaty councils. They were suspicious about his presence, thinking that he would influence the proceedings in some way; they therefore refused to speak to him, and Ramsey advised him to go home. Finally, on September 22, Little Boy, a head warrior, spoke to Hole-in-the-Day in council, expressing the Red Lakers reservations about him, particularly the rumors they had heard that he was in league with the hostile Sioux led by Little Crow:

> **My nephew: I have a few words to say to you. Last winter, when the messenger came through on his way to Pembina, I said that the government need never fear that the Red Lakers would join the Sioux to fight the whites. That the whites thought that the Red Lakers were siding with you during your raid at Crow Wing...was false. There is not a single instance where we raised a hand against the white man. The white man has always supported us....We do not do as you have done, go and shake hands with the Sioux, and then come back and shake hands with the white man. We never would assist you nor any other man to raise hands against the white people, and we do not want such a notion to be abroad.**
>
> **My nephew, we have heard that you were coming here for the sake of raising trouble amongst us. We have heard from the prairies that you were in correspondence with Little Crow and his bands. We want it distinctly understood that we want nothing to do with you or with your plans....**

Hole-in-the-Day responded that "whoever said these things were liars," and the council broke up.

Source: [Alexander Ramsey] *Miscellaneous Pamphlets*, Vol. 2, no. 25

"....I see gold glittering on the soil we inherit."

LITTLE ROCK **September 26, 1863**

AFTER THE ISSUE of Hole-in-the-Day's presence was settled, the U.S. commissioners continued to press the Red Lake chiefs for a treaty. The government wanted title to the Red River valley, on both sides of the river (an estimated 20,000 square miles), and was willing to pay $20,000 per year for twenty years. The Red Lakers appointed Little Rock, a chief of one of their bands, to speak for them. After shaking hands with Ramsey and Morrill, he spoke, according to a reporter, "with somewhat undue violence of vociferation, but with neither immoderate nor ungraceful energy of gesticulation." Paul Beaulieu interpreted for the chief, who said:

> Whenever I look around I see and I suppose you see it also--I see gold glittering on the soil we inherit. The land belongs to us. We should be very sorry for you to set a value upon the land for us and make us an offer...before you have heard our offer.
>
> I want to give you an answer to one thing you said yesterday--about the road which passes through here and the river. You told us they were not of much importance to us. The Master of Life gave us the river and the water thereof to drink, and the woods and the roads we depend on for subsistence, and you are mistaken if you think we derive no benefits from them. The Master of Life gave it to us for an inheritance, and gave us the animals for food and clothing....
>
> About the road and that river which flows in that direction, which the Master of Life has given me--there is where I get my living. My independence is upon that prairie. The Master of Life has placed upon these prairies animals from which I live. Their meat is my food, and their skins are my clothing. It seems now that the white man is passing backward and forward and wresting these prairies from our hands, and taking this food from my mouth.
>
> My friend, when we take anything which has been left upon the ground, even though it be of small value, we feel bad. We are afraid to look the owner in the face until we restore it. Now about committing depredations and stealing, we are well aware that the Great Spirit has given us the animals for our support. When your young men steal anything you make them pay for the depredations. That is the way we look upon those white men who drove away the animals and fish the Great Spirit has given us....
>
> Do you suppose we are ignorant that the amount of money you offer us is a mere handful and would not go but a little way towards paying for what I think you alluded to (compensation for depredations)....We want you to distinctly understand that the proposition you made to us yesterday ($20,000 for the right of way) we don't accept. We do not think of it at all....

Despite the initial determination of the band to resist the sale, the commissioners eventually had their way and the treaty was signed by six of the seven Red Lake chiefs.

Source: *St. Paul Daily Press*, October 23, 1863. "May-dwa-gun-onind [He Who is Spoken To], a tall, noble-looking and keen-faced Indian, is the head chief of the Red Lakers, but like other great men talking is not his forte. Little Rock, his more than peer in stature and in influence, a man of character with a massive brow and an intelligent and open face, is the orator and statesman of the Red Lake hierarchy, functions which the Pembinese devolve on old Red Bear." *St. Paul Daily Press*, October 4, 1863.

"...but the way our lands were disposed of [it] looks as if we were robbed...."

HE WHO IS SPOKEN TO — October 14, 1863

THE HEAD CHIEF OF THE RED LAKERS, He Who is Spoken To, was broken-hearted over the treaty his people made with the government (and which he hadn't signed.) He wrote to Bishop Whipple to say that his people did not wish to withhold their lands from the Great Father, "but the way our lands were disposed of [it] looks as if we were robbed of our property." He wanted to visit Washington to complain.

Whipple considered the chief to be a man "of far more than ordinary intelligence. A man who is truthful, and who feels the deepest solicitude for his people, and one of those who fears and deeply feels the dread of that destruction which seems to await his people." Later that year, He Who is Spoken To journeyed one hundred miles during the winter to see Whipple at Leech Lake. He said that he was heart-sick and unable to sleep since the treaty was made; that it had been made only to please the traders and that no provision was made for schools, seed, homes, or farms: "They had only a little money and that would soon go; that if they were to remain wild men and live by the chase, they were fools to sell their lands, which were now their hunting grounds." The chief then drew the boundaries of his land in the ashes of a fire and remarked:

> **There is my country. I am a wild man, and live by the chase; I kill the elk, the moose, and the deer, and my wife builds my lodge and gathers the wild rice and catches fish. When your white brothers come here, there will be no elk, no deer, no moose. I shall have a little reservation to die upon. I hear we are to be removed. Go tell your people I have so many warriors whose shadows rest on their graves.**

He warned further that seven-eighths of his people were dissatisfied with the treaty and that blood would have been shed if he had not prevented it. Whipple endorsed the chief's request to be allowed to go to Washington. In March 1864 the chief, along with his two brothers, Leading Feather and Straight Bird, as well as Little Rock, and the Pembina chief Red Bear, made a new treaty.

Sources: Henry Whipple to William P. Dole, Nov. 24, 1863, OIA, LR, Chippewa Agency; Henry B. Whipple, "Bishop Whipple's Report on the Moral and Temporal Condition of the Indian Tribes on our Western Border," ca. 1868, in Whipple Papers, MHS; *St. Cloud Democrat*, March 10, 1864.

"...we have only a stone's throw that is good for anything...."

HOLE-IN-THE-DAY October 29, 1863

A NUMBER OF MISSISSIPPI OJIBWAY chiefs met with Governor Ramsey in October 1863 to persuade him to endorse their request to go to Washington to make a new treaty. Various chiefs spoke, including Berry Picker of Sandy Lake (who was Hole-in-the-Day's uncle), Little Frenchman of Pokegama, and Feather's End of Mille Lacs. Paul Beaulieu was the interpreter and Benjamin Thompson the recorder. Berry Picker explained that he wanted Hole-in-the-Day and his son, Red Turtle, to represent their bands in Washington. Then Hole-in-the-Day spoke:

> It has pleased the Master of Life to let us meet a person we are all glad to see, that our Great Father has sent to us. What we speak of today are subjects of the greatest importance to us; they are matters of life and death to us. Father and friend, what these old men say to you are the sentiments of all of us....I am sorry that by the terms of the treaty no clause was left so that we would be allowed to amend it. The consideration of these things makes it a matter of life or death to us, for when we look at the treaty, we have only a stone's throw that is good for anything, and we see no way of bettering ourselves.
>
> We hope that you will use your influence for us. We respect the government, and wish our Great Father to make it better for us. We speak to you, and we wish to say to you that we do not flatter, but we have known you a great while, and we all know you have a great deal of influence, as you should have, here, and with our Great Father, and we ask you to do what you can to help us.
>
> I must not now be misunderstood. I might say much more, but I must shield myself. If I have ever committed any errors, I wish to correct them, and my young men all feel the same way. I am willing to sacrifice myself for my band, and die for them....We are all like sick men and you are our doctor.

By March 1864 Hole-in-the-Day and Red Turtle were on their way to Washington, in company with the Red Lake chiefs who also were planning to make a new treaty. Hole-in-the-Day's treaty was signed on May 7, and by it, the old reservations were given up for a reserve north and west of Leech Lake. Again, however, the Ojibways felt that they had given up their reserves for a mere pittance; and Ignatius Donnelly, one of Minnesota's famous politicians, claimed that the old reservations were a "garden spot" compared to the new "sterile location" that had been chosen. Still, the treaty was ratified. However, before removal took place, Hole-in-the-Day was ready to make yet another treaty in place of it.

Sources: *[Ramsey] Miscellaneous Pamphlets*, 46-48; *St. Cloud Democrat*, May 19, 1864. Berry Picker, or Berry Hunter (Kahnundahwahwenzo), was a son of Chief Broken Tooth, born in about 1800. His sister, Mahnun, was married to the elder Chief Hole-in-the-Day. Berry Hunter died in the 1880s and was succeeded as chief by his son, Red Turtle (Misquadace), who died in about 1900.

"...if we should all get together again, some of us will have to bite the dust...."

SHABASHKUNG August 21, 1864

SHABASHKUNG, or He That Passes Under Everything, became the leading Mille Lacs Ojibway chief in the 1860s. According to a white observer, Shabashkung was "a fine looking, smart, shrewd Indian. His features are more sharp than the usual Indian caste, with a Roman nose, a keen eye, and...much more than ordinary intelligence and discrimination; talks fluently and generally to the point. On this occasion he wore a fine black cloth coat, cloth leggins, and red blanket. He exercises quite a controlling influence over the other chiefs."

The Mille Lacs Ojibway had been forced for some years to obtain their annuities at Crow Wing, which by 1864 was a center of the whiskey trade. The chiefs began to complain that their people were worse off after they got their annuities than before, for the reason that their money was spent on whiskey--and, they said, "if we do not buy whiskey at Crow Wing, the people bring it to us on the road, get us drunk and take everything we have." Fearing not only the loss of their money, but also the loss of life which might result if they continued to get their annuities at Crow Wing, Shabashkung dictated the following letter to superintendent Clark Thompson; it was translated and written down by Peter Roy:

> Some time early this summer we went and saw Major Morrill and asked him to have our share of the annuities brought to us at Mille Lac....We hear from different persons that Agent Morrill would not help us....
>
> I am very sorry to know that we Mille Lac bands, who are so friendly to the whites, and [who] tried to do what is just and right, that we shall always be served at the very last.
>
> I hope my friend that you will see the necessity of getting our annuities at Mille Lac. [In the] first place, it costs us good for having going and [coming] back, and we lost the very best time for hunting and putting up fish for our winter use, and again you know how it is--an Indian for fire water, he spent his last cent for it, and sell[s] his shirt off his back....You know there is about forty killed since the last time....no doubt if we should all get together again, some [of] us will have to bite the dust again....

Thompson endorsed the request to the commissioner of Indian affairs, saying that "we are under obligation to them for the influences they exerted...in putting down the attempted raid of Hole-in-the-Day."

Shabashkung, as a speaker, was quickwitted and good with short retorts. When a commissioner tried to persuade him to remove to the new reservation, arguing that he was "fifty-five winters" old and had a silvered gray head and had never done any wrong to anyone, the chief replied: "Look at me, the winds of fifty-five winters have blown over my head, and have silvered it over with gray, but -- they have not blown my brains away! I have done." At an 1866 annuity payment, the chief told agent Edwin Clark: "We call you our father from courtesy, but we know you are not our father, else we would be nearer one color!"

Sources: Shabashkung to Clark Thompson, August 21, 1864, OIA, LR, Chippewa Agency; M. C. Levi, *Chippewa Indians of Yesterday and Today* (New York: Pageant Press, Inc., 1956), 6-7; *St. Cloud Journal*, Nov. 15 and Dec. 13, 1866.

"We have suffered enough. Our cup is full."

HOLE-IN-THE-DAY January 1, 1867

AFFAIRS AMONG THE MISSISSIPPI OJIBWAYS were in a deplorable state in the mid-1860s. The Indians' corn crops were not always successful, and some years the wild rice crop failed, and even the rabbit population, which often subsisted the Ojibways, had diminished to the point that few could be obtained. Hole-in-the-Day blamed the recent agents for compounding their problems. He fought for the removal of Edwin Clark (agent from 1865-66), and was no happier about Clark's successor, Joel B. Bassett, a Minneapolis businessman. There were numerous reports, even by prominent whites, that Bassett conducted a corrupt administration. Oscar Taylor reported to Bishop Whipple (in 1867): "...I am satisfied that there has never been so much stealing and imposition at any time as during the last year." John Johnson reported that the agent has "stain on his hands that can be proven against him by men here. I considered him the very worst agent that we ever have [had]--no comparison to Major [David] Herriman, who robbed the poor Indian everything he could." No wonder then that Hole-in-the-Day dictated the following letter to O. H. Browning, the secretary of the interior, on January 1, 1867:

> **My father: nearly six months ago I wrote to your office in regard to our present agent, Mr. Edwin Clark, informing you of his disability or lack of abilities to control or manage our affairs; thus unnecessary difficulties arise giving dissatisfaction not only to the Indians, but also to the white inhabitants.**
>
> **Last fall [1866] I received encouragement from Senator [Daniel S.] Norton, that there should be a change made in this office. I have waited patiently, but alas, I have been disappointed had I have supposed this I should certainly have visited you ere this, and laid my grievances, which are many, at your feet. When I saw that this man was to continue I felt sorely grieved for my people, and could only say --why have I been thus deceived....In conversation only yesterday I remarked to our agent that up to this time I had not attempted to oppose him, but said I from this time until you are removed I am your enemy and unless you leave us, trouble must follow.**
>
> **It is not often I write to you; I dislike to trouble you, but my heart is full and I write as I feel and think, and nothing but the truth. We have suffered enough. Our cup is full. If we are to perish, it matters not how.**
>
> **Report says Mr. Joel Bassett is to be our next agent. I would ask what is the difference between these men; they are one and the same, and I feel certain his appointment will only be a repetition of what we have had from Clark.**
>
> **Now, my father, do not think lightly of my words. I am speaking the sentiments of 6,000 poor needy people; they are all your children, and look to you for protection, and if you slight us, to whom can we go, where can we look? Pity us, my father, and give us an agent who knows our ways, and will be kind and generous to us, and the Great Spirit will watch kindly over you.**
>
> **Your sincere friend,**
> **Hole-in-the-Day, Chippewa chief**

Sources: Hole-in-the-Day to O.H. Browning, Jan. 1, 1867, Joel Bassett Papers, MHS; Oscar Taylor to Bishop Whipple, Nov. 13, 1867, John Johnson to Whipple, Nov. 26, 1867, Whipple Papers.

"Somebody wants a big contract with big figures."

HOLE-IN-THE-DAY **August 19, 1867**

AFTER THE WHITE EARTH RESERVATION was established by treaty in 1867, Hole-in-the-Day was a leading opponent of removal to it. He objected to the fact that promised improvements upon it had not been made. However, agent Bassett strongly pushed removal for the reason that he apparently stood to gain financially through a scheme with a contractor, who was supposed to provide the Ojibways a total of $105,000 worth of services and goods. Bishop Whipple was particularly dismayed over suspicions about Bassett because he had helped to place Bassett in office; he was later to write: "So profitable are these harvests of iniquity that in a recent removal of the Chippewas, over $20,000 was paid to secure the contract to provide rations for the Indians." Hole-in-the-Day, having exhausted all conventional avenues for redress, wrote an anonymous letter to the editor of a St. Paul paper, questioning the push for removal to White Earth:

> Why are they so fast to give a contract for our subsistence? This ought to be the last thing to be done. I have some idea why they want to give the contract at this early date. Somebody wants a big contract with big figures. The provisions are very high at this present time, but are bound to come down to 50 to 100 per cent within three or four months.
>
> We hope that our Great Father will not demand our removal before he makes his promise good. We want our farms open and our houses built and a saw mill and roads. When this is done, we are willing to leave our old homes and go to our new reservation....
>
> In regard to the Mille Lac bands, there is not a dollar yet appropriated towards their removal, and the government has agreed to let them remain...as long as they are friendly and peaceable with the whites. Now what have they done that they should be required to remove---because that [a] few of them go down to the settlements and kill deer? Have they not as good [a] right to kill deer as the settlers? But the settlers do not want to see the Indians kill deer; they think because an Indian has sold his country that he has no right to hunt on it. If they know anything at all, they ought to know that the Indians are subjects of the United States, and have just as good a right to hunt on government land [as] a white man. Where is there a white man that makes his business in hunting, that does hunt on his own land? Not one. We hope that the Mille Lac Indians will not be required to remove at this time. They are peaceable, friendly, and industrious bands of Indians.
>
> We would like to see the Commissioner of Indian Affairs at the Chippewa Agency, where all the chief warriors and young men can be seen present, to have a better understanding with our Great Father in regard to our removal....We are as a tribe of the Chippewas have always been, on friendly terms with the whites, and we would always like to be. We demand of the white settlers of Minnesota not to be too fast to demand our removal. Give us time. God knows that the Indians will not be in the way of the whites many years to come. I am,
>
> CHIPPEWA OF MISSISSIPPI BANDS.

Sources: *St. Paul Pioneer*, August 27, 1867; Bishop Whipple's Report on the Moral and Temporal Condition of the Indian Tribes on our Western Border, ca. 1868, Whipple Papers.

"I am afraid, father, that you are making...business in the dark corner."

WHITE FISHER September 1867

WHITE FISHER, the elderly Gull Lake chief, joined Hole-in-the-Day in the protest against premature removal of the Ojibways to White Earth. He was one of the great warriors of the Mississippi bands, having earlier served as a war chief for the elder Hole-in-the-Day. William Warren reported that, by 1852, White Fisher could boast of having survived nine wounds inflicted upon him by the Sioux (however, he had lost two children and five brothers and sisters killed). In September 1867, the chief went to speak with agent Joel Bassett regarding the motives behind the push to remove his people. John Johnson translated and recorded the speech.

I am a man. I have followed the war path. When I do anything, I do it openly and publicly, what is in my heart. [I have] more right [to speak] than any of my fellow chiefs [because] traders did not make me [a] chief, as most of my fellow chiefs....My people and one of your big chief[s] from Washington, [a] great many winters ago, made my father [Bedud] chief, and for this reason I say I have [a] right to speak with you on this present occasion.

Father, I understand that you are about to move us this fall to our new reservation. I want to tell you plainly--Where did you take the chiefs to go and select their country? How many have you taken, and what improvement have you made for us [at] our new homes according to the agreement made between our Great Father and us?

Why is it that you are so [much] in [a] hurry to move us? We are ready and willing to move at any time when the promises are fulfilled in the treaty--not before.

Father, do hear me. I say, and on behalf of all my people, I will not move, nor any of my people, this fall. I am afraid, father, that you are making, or doing, business in the dark corner, and [are] throwing something into our faces that we cannot see what you are doing. If it came from [a] good heart, and [from] pity[ing] us, you never would be so hasty about moving us. There is something that you are after--[but] not for the good of your children; and if you insist on moving us, I want to shake hands with you once more and with a strong hand, I say I am a man, and feel like a man!

Source: Enmegahbowh (John Johnson) to Whipple, September 13, 1867, Whipple Papers. On suspected corruption by Bassett, see C. A. Ruffee to Whipple, October 8, 1867, and Whipple to Bassett, Nov. 14, 1867, Whipple Papers. This White Fisher was not related to the White Fisher of the eighteenth century. The first White Fisher was the son of Big Feet, and this White Fisher was the son of Bedud, and grandson of Noka.

"The white man does not scalp the head, but he poisons the heart...."

LITTLE THUNDER **circa Spring 1868**

A GROUP OF MISSIONARIES visited the Red Lake Ojibway in 1868, including one Dr. Prescott. During their stay, Prescott read from the Gospel of Matthew to a number of Indian listeners; he covered a portion regarding the story of a servant who was forgiven a debt by his master, but then refused to likewise forgive a debt to a fellow servant. An Ojibway named Little Thunder commented:

> **White men are seldom good. Indians would be ashamed to do what they do. The white man does not scalp the head, but he poisons the heart, and that is worse. Gitchee Ogema [the great chief] Lincoln was good, and there are some like him; but a white man killed him, and the man the book [the Bible] talks to you of, was also killed, because he was good. The white man does not love goodness. His heart is bad.**

Source: Helen C. Weeks (Campbell), *White and Red; A Narrative of Life Among the Northwest Indians.* (New York: Hurd and Houghton Cambridge Press, 1869), 185-86.

"I see salvation for my children in that place--White Earth...."

NEBUNESHKUNG June 4, 1868

BY JUNE 1868 many of the Mississippi Ojibways were anxious to move to White Earth regardless of the improvements promised by the treaty of 1867. They were prompted mostly by the fact that the whiskey trade at Crow Wing had caused a great number of deaths due to drunken brawls. Still, a number of the Ojibways led by Hole-in-the-Day were opposed to removal until the government had fulfilled its responsibilities on the new reserve. By early June the division among the bands was pronounced. Nebuneshkung, who had been a leading warrior, headed up the faction that was determined to go to White Earth; he was supported by chiefs Manitowab and White Cloud (the son of Chief White Fisher). On June 4 they formed a caravan with eleven ox teams and two hundred people, including the interpreters, Paul Beaulieu and Truman Warren. Hole-in-the-Day's men, however, stood in the road, determined to stop their departure, threatening to kill the first man to pass them. But Nebuneshkung was undeterred. He drew his butcher knife and proclaimed:

> **My people are looking in a grave. If we go to this new country we shall be saved. You say you will kill any man who goes to White Earth. You know me--I am going to White Earth, and I will kill any man who would murder me.**
>
> **I see salvation for my children in that place--White Earth--and I see it nowhere else. I will bury this knife in the breast of the first man who attempts to stop me from saving my children--be he whom he may!**

Hole-in-the-Day's men backed down, allowing the caravan to pass. The chief figured it would be better to take his complaints to Washington. However, the day before he was to leave, he was assassinated by Pillager warriors, who had been hired by prominent mixed-bloods of Crow Wing (They were upset because Hole-in-the-Day had wanted to keep them off the new reserve.) Nebuneshkung and his following arrived at White Earth on June 14, 1868; other Ojibways followed that winter. The old warrior, also known as Isaac Tuttle, died of consumption in 1874.

Sources: Whipple, *Lights and Shadows*, 263; J. A. Gilfillan, "Nebuneshkunk, the Ideal Soldier," *The Red Man* (Carlisle, PA: Jan. 1913), 195; John Johnson to Whipple, Jan. 6, 1868, Whipple Papers; Diedrich, *Chiefs Hole-in-the-Day*, 46-48.

HE WHO IS SPOKEN TO

CHAPTER EIGHT

THE GREAT POVERTY, 1874-1889

"You see that I am now nothing but a corpse...."

"...I dare fearlessly to point to the future...."

WHITE CLOUD June 20, 1874

IN JUNE 1874 the Ojibways of White Earth celebrated the sixth anniversary of their arrival at their new reservation in northwestern Minnesota. According to a reporter, "the feature of the affair par excellence was the speech of White Cloud" --who became the most prominent chief of the Mississippi bands after the deaths of White Fisher and Hole-in-the-Day. The reporter said further, that the speech was "worthy of preservation as a model of eloquence and native conception." Translation was not given at the time, so that White Cloud was able to give "full vent to his powers," he thus "carried away all with him by the passion of his sentiments." Paul Beaulieu later provided translation. The chief's words reflect the influence upon him of the Christianity preached by the Protestant Episcopal missionaries, and Bishop Whipple himself. Proclaiming that "the ignorance of the past" had been changed "for the wisdom and enlightenment of the present and the future," he said:

> **Should I refer to our lost possessions, the loss of which has soured the disposition of the Indian race in general toward those whom they look on as the cause of all their misery, and which has turned their once noble natures like to beasts of prey. I would do wrong to the mandates of the Master of Life. His words are, "Love thy neighbor as thyself." And what more sympathy do you want? You have the sympathy of the Christian world....**
>
> **Six years ago this day we arrived at this place, making in our history a page most eventful. By the advice of one of the greatest friends that was ever known to the Chippewa [Bishop Whipple], we submitted our future into the hands of our Heavenly Father. Need I remind you of the result? When we were menaced with difficulties from whence came the good advice, trust to God? Now open your eyes and see and behold the holy church, by the which comfort is given you. While under the dominion of King Alcohol, where was your trust?**
>
> **....I dare not refer to the past, much less draw a picture of the same for fear that your stoicism should forsake you. But I dare fearlessly to point to the future, taking as a basis what has been wrought for you during the past six years. Your destiny is in your hands. Uncompromising faith, steadiness in your purpose, a willingness to bear the penalty of man's sins--"By the sweat of thy brow shalt thou eat thy daily bread," and anxious willingness to strictly adhere to the teachings of those that the Master of Life has been pleased to send to redeem you--adhere to those principles and you are all right....**

The chief closed with a request that they all remember "the Moses of our Exodus" (Bishop Whipple) and their "Aaron " (John Johnson). And following his own advice, he sent his son, Nashotah (Charles Wright), to attend school at Fairbault --afterwards becoming an ordained Episcopal priest.

Sources: *St. Paul Dispatch*, June 26, 1874; *St. Paul Daily Globe*, February 10, 1878.

"...if you do not help us, we will die in our poverty."

FLAT MOUTH (II), LITTLE ROCK, and WHITE CLOUD 1877

EACH SUMMER from 1873 through 1877, a disasterous cloud of locusts invaded the Minnesota farm country, devouring almost everything green in sight. By the winter of 1876-77 the situation was drastically affecting the Ojibway reservations in northern Minnesota. Various chiefs began to write to their foremost influential friend, Bishop Henry Whipple, for assistance. Flat Mouth II wrote from Leech Lake on January 13, 1877:

> **My people are starving and freezing, and no work is being done for us. We received at our annual payment a very few goods, and our children are consequently suffering. Within the last two or three years the administration of our affairs have been such as to show no improvement, and we appear in a worse condition than formerly. We desire you to write to Washington to explain our situation and to control our affairs.**

A month later Whipple received a letter from Little Rock on the Red Lake reserve:

> **Our friend, we met in council today--[and] thought of you in our necessities. You are our friend and you are one whom we know would help us. You know very well our poverty. We have never had any help since we went to see our Great Father at Washington and we would like very much to go and see him once more before our annuities expire, and thought only of you who would help us to go on, and we wish to borrow money from you out of monies due us from the government next fall, or sooner, if we get help from our Great Father....We wish to bear our own expenses. If you can help us in this matter, it will show us that you are our friend....if you do not help us, we will die in our poverty. You know we cannot follow any religion naked. We must have help from our Great Father.**

Then, in May 1877, Whipple heard from White Cloud at the White Earth reserve:

> **When you were here last summer, you saw the grasshoppers, and now their children are among us, threatening to destroy everything again this year as they did last. The last time I saw you, you said you would come here soon and see us again. I looked and watched for you, but you came not. I afterwards heard that the Great Father had sent you to see the Sioux and heard of the success of your work among them. I would like to have you write and advise me in my new mode of life. Maybe you may not think me worthy, but I shall deem it my duty to advise my people.**

Sources: Flat Mouth to Whipple, Jan. 13, 1877, Red Lake chiefs to Whipple, Feb. 13, 1877, and White Cloud to Whipple, May 18, 1877, Whipple Papers. One result of the complaints was that the White Earth agent, Lewis Stowe was replaced by the old trader and mail route operator, Charles A. Ruffee. White Cloud's activities in getting Stowe replaced caused missionary J. A. Gilfillan to give him a poor historical reputation. See Frederick W. Hodge, ed. *Handbook of American Indians*, Part 2 (Totowa, NJ: Rowman and Littlefield, 1979), 885.

"I am afraid of that paper--it appears to me like a match to burn up our country."

MOOSEMANI March 22, 1880

BY THE 1880S, Moosemani, or Moose, was a leading chief among the Mille Lacs Ojibways, along with old Shabashkung. He was born in the mid-1820s, and fought in several battles with the Sioux, including the 1842 attack led by Hole-in-the-Day, the Elder, on the Little Crow village near St. Paul, and the 1858 battle at Shakopee. In 1863 Moosemani accompanied Shabashkung, Rat's Liver, and Rice Maker on a trip to Washington. When his father died (Rice Maker ?), Moosemani became chief of a Mille Lacs band which resided on the southeast side of the lake (Shabashkung and his band lived on the northwest side.) Nathan Richardson (of Little Falls) described the chief in 1880 as being a "quite large, muscular, and well-built man."

The Mille Lacs Ojibways always boasted of their friendship to the whites, particularly at the time of Hole-in-the-Day's hostile demonstrations at Crow Wing in 1862. They expected in return that the whites would treat them with due consideration. However, in early 1880 they heard rumors that by some means their reservation no longer belonged to them; and in fact, bogus entries had been made in the Taylor's Falls land office regarding the sale of Indian pine lands. Moosemani headed up a delegation of chiefs and headmen to present their complaints before the people of Little Falls on March 22, 1880. With Peter Roy interpreting, the chief spoke of the effort made by some unknown party to drive them from their reserve; that they desired to see the Great Father, but were "chained up":

> **When the treaty [of 1863] was made with my father and other men who are now dead, we think they made provision for us, their children. I am afraid of that paper [in the land office] --it appears to me like a match to burn up our country.**
>
> **My friends, I may not be able to speak eloquently, but I am afraid of that paper, and I appeal to you...to give us a helping hand. My father helped make the treaty, and before he died he called me and asked me to preserve and keep the reservation.**

Moosemani then presented a petition addressed to President Rutherford B. Hayes, which said in part:

> **We hear that many false accusations have been made against us, and sent to our Great Father. If such is the case, we hope he will not be deceived by them....if we prove ourselves innocent, we shall ask for a new treaty, or that the one we now have be made definite and perfect, so that pine land thieves will not dare to come upon our reservation, as they have done in the past, and take our timber from us without our consent.... We therefore humbly ask and urge upon you to listen to our appeal to you for justice, and ask that you and our kind friend, Carl Shurz...may without delay take such action as shall make us secure in our rights and home forever....**

Sources: Little Falls *Daily Transcript*, April 9 and 16, 1880. Again, in 1883, Moosemani and Shabashkung endeavored to protect their homes against settlers who wanted land under the "soldiers' additional homestead act." At their request, Governor Lucius Hubbard promised to send an agent to investigate the matter. See Minneapolis *Daily Tribune*, July 18, 1883. Historically, Moosemani is known due to a crazy mixup concerning a monument erected at Fort Ridgely in 1914. If the Mille Lacs Ojibways were to be honored for not becoming hostile to the whites in 1862, the monument should have been erected near Fort Ripley, or Mille Lacs. Furthermore, Moosemani was only a member of the Mille Lacs bands at the time, not a chief; and so the monument should have more properly mentioned the names of chiefs, like Shabashkung. See "Monument to Mouzoomaunee," in William W. Folwell, *A History of Minnesota* 4 vols. (St. Paul: Minnesota Historical Society, 1921-30), 2:382.

"...I saw his blood on the ground...."

SHABASHKUNG July 20, 1881

ON JULY 17, 1881, two whites who had been drinking, visited an Ojibway camp near Aitkin, Minnesota, and promiscuously fired guns at the Indians. Quakegeshig, the brother of Shabashkung, who was a chief, was killed! Two hundred and fifty armed Ojibways quickly descended upon the town of Aitkin to demand life for life. The two men who had committed the murder had been taken into custody by the local sheriff. On July 19 Shabashkung arrived on the scene, and demanded that the prisoners be delivered over to him for punishment. Although the officials refused this request, they agreed to allow the chief to accompany the prisoners on the trip to St. Paul and promised him a meeting with Governor John S. Pillsbury.

On July 20 Shabashkung arose to speak to the governor, with Joseph Robert interpreting. The chief was described as being sixty-five to seventy years old, five feet eleven and a half inches in height, tall and sparely built: "His eye is keen and his oratory earnest if not eloquent. He wore a blanket and the usual Indian dress, leggins, moccasins, etc., but was devoid of the usual head dress due to one of his rank." The chief announced pointedly that he wanted to know what would be done about the killing of his brother, and continuing, said:

> **When three days ago I heard that my brother, who had gone out from his people on a visit to the white settlement, had been killed, I would not believe it; but when I came to the spot where it was done, and I saw his blood upon the ground, I knew he was dead!**
>
> **I have always tried to do what was right, what was good, with the whites. So with my brother. My brother had done nothing wrong to the bad men who had killed him. He had not been drinking, or doing anything to create a disturbance or bad feeling. As my brother had always been good, I do not want his killing to rest where it is.**
>
> **I told the officer here and others before we left Aitkin [that] the bad men who killed my brother must be punished. The young braves want revenge. But we have always behaved and kept peace with the whites as we promised the Great White Father at Washington we would.... When Hole-in-the-Day tried to get us to make war upon the whites, we told him no! So we feel today. We only ask the same justice we mete out. When an Indian killed a half-breed at Little Rock Lake, we held a council and decided the murderer must die....and we carried out our sentence. This is what we want you to do with the men who killed my brother....**

Governor Pillsbury promised that the men would be punished just the same as if they had killed a white man.

Source: *St. Paul Daily Globe*, July 21, 1881.

"...I am but a child; I suck the teat of ignorance...."

WHITE CLOUD August 6, 1886

IN THE SUMMER OF 1885, Minnesota settlers began to demand that the White Earth Reservation be opened up to white settlement; businessmen of the logging interests wanted to harvest the Ojibway's rich timber crop. Bishop Henry Whipple protested on behalf of the tribe, but a plan was developed to consolidate the other Ojibway bands at White Earth. Whipple felt that the consolidation would save the wandering, poor Ojibway of the other reserves, and keep White Earth intact. He received an appointment as a commissioner of the "Northwest Commission." Six days of council were held at White Earth in early August 1886. Whipple said that the Great Father would make the poor Ojibways rich when they agreed to move to White Earth and take up allotments of land. White Cloud was selected by the White Earth people as their "principal talker" to respond to the commission. Paul Beaulieu was the interpreter. White Cloud agreed to the proposal, but not without some fear and misgiving:

> ....While we were here, at a loss and not knowing what would become of us, and hoping for the future, you have opened before us, as it were, the daylight....Through infancy and until we grew to be youths all these you see in here before you, listened to their parents of the past, men who have long since passed away. They told us of the past life of our people, they told us what our future would be, and those prophecies have come to pass. They told us that the day would come when we would be surrounded by the whites. They told us of the strength of the whites, and everything they told us is coming to pass this very day. Now, when we think of the future, and look at our children and know our own weakness, know that we are children in the eyes of the whites, it is with fear that we live....When I look around me I do not know which way to fly. Retreat is impossible....
>
> It was with truth that our bishop uttered the words that he did of a great many years ago when he first saw us.... You are the man who took us from the dust. You are the man who shook the dust away from us. You are the man that put us again on our feet....From year to year when we see the actions of the whites, how they are looking upon our land with covetous eyes, that would willingly take us and anchor us to the bottom of the sea, you, Bishop Whipple, still stand by us and uphold us. I know my weakness; I know my ignorance; I cannot compete with the whites....By your help we acquired this reservation; it was well understood that this was to be the future homes of the Indians of the Mississippi band; it was understood that we should never be removed from here. Remember, my friends, this is the last of all our possessions....
>
> We will open our reservations to all persons of Chippewa blood; we open it with that feeling, that you will extend to us a helping hand and make this a permanent arrangement....There are men who are too fast--I may get muddled; I have no understanding; I am but a child; I suck the teat of ignorance, and that ignorance may adhere to me forever. Do not push me too fast forward....

Sources: Chippewa Indians in Minnesota, in 49 Congress, 2 Session, *Senate Executive Document*, no. 115, Vol. 2, 1887 (serial 2449), 59-60; Folwell, *History of Minnesota*, 4:198-207.

"It would be just like holding a hatchet over the heads and one of us slaughtered every day...."

SHOKAHGESHIG September 15, 1886

MANY OJIBWAYS were skeptical of the words spoken by the Northwest Commission; they did not need to look too far back to find broken and unfulfilled promises. Shokahgeshig spoke for the Winnibigoshish Ojibway band (which lived north of the Pillager bands of Leech Lake) at Raven's Point:

> **We do not know whether the Great Father has fulfilled all his promises or not with us, but we know that a great many things that we have had promised us have never reached us; and they [the Ojibways] have said this, that they are afraid that this same thing may happen again.**
>
> **We view it in the right light--what the commission is saying to us as a very great and good arrangement for us; it looks well and sounds well; but we are afraid that the same thing will happen again that has happened before.**
>
> **It seems to us that if we were all gathered on one reservation, that life would not last more than a day; it seems as though it would be sickly to have so many of us there. It would be just like holding a hatchet over the heads and one of us slaughtered every day....**

Source: *Chippewa Indians in Minnesota,* 117.

"I wish rather that my bones shall bleach out on the shores of this lake."

SHABASHKUNG October--November 1886

THE MILLE LACS BAND put up strong resistance against the proposed removal to White Earth. It became evident that the stance the Mille Lacs Ojibway had taken against the Hole-in-the-Day revolt of 1862 had seriously disrupted the relations between them and the Mississippi bands. Shabashkung was especially resentful that Chief Crossing Sky accompanied the commissioners, and was referring to the Mille Lacs Ojibways as "Mississippi people." At a council on October 11, held at the outlet to the Rum River, Shabashkung spoke to Crossing Sky:

> ...we see in your actions that you do not reach anything out on your fork to us. You do not give us even cow dung to sit on. You moved away from here. We know why you left us; you could not stir us up when you tried to excite against the whites you are traveling with. As you see yonder lake, calm and placid, so are the hearts of those braves; these Mille Lacs Indians are good Indians. Do not term us hereafter Mississippi Indians, but different....
>
> [Turning to the commissioners] They are satisfied to stay here where they have lived in poverty. We have pity for ourselves and for our dead, and wish not to leave them. I wish rather that my bones shall bleach out on the shores of this lake....These young men have made up their minds to sit quiet under all persecutions that may fall upon them from the whites....They [the president and commissioner] told us we might stay here a thousand years if we wished to....

Moosemani added: "Is the one thousand years up that the Great Father sent you here....I was a young man when the white men first began to ask us for our lands. Now you can see by my head how old I am...." At a second council on November 3, 1886, Bishop Whipple pleaded for Shabashkung's agreement to the proposal, saying that "wise men never grow miserable over the past," but "look to the future." The band was offered $25,000 in consideration for the promises that they could remain at Mille Lacs. Shabashkung, however, would not give in, saying:

> My friends, never in my life have I done anything to give cause for my not shaking hands with you, and I have worked hard to keep these people from doing anything wrong. It has been hard for me to fight to keep them straight. It has been up and down, and I am tired out. I have used all my power and influence for the good of these Mille Lacs Indians, and I don't see what I have gained....
>
> And now, my friends, I just say this: Let me live in peace on my own land....I want to stay here with my sons...I have been fifty years gardening and digging the ground up with my hands and...still I am making enough to live upon. I am very old, as you can see, but I am not afraid that I shall die of starvation....

Source: Chippewa Indians in Minnesota, 35-37.

"...undo persuasion was used to get many to sign the so-called agreement who bitterly regret it today."

WHITE CLOUD February 1888

WHITE CLOUD signed the treaty of 1886 for the Northwest Commission, headed by Bishop Whipple. However, he later felt that the Ojibways had been unfairly pressured into signing it, and therefore wished it to be abrogated. He gave the following statement to a reporter for the White Earth Agency newspaper:

> I am strongly opposed to the agreement for many reasons, and principally against the Common Fund Plan. I consider that the commissioner took undo advantage of the Indians. In the first place, a sufficient length of time was not given to them to consider a matter of so much importance as the agreement was to them. It was a big thing.
>
> The commission had certain propositions to them, and they [the Ojibways] had no alternative but to accept or reject them, and seemingly having no voice in the matter to do this. Bishop Whipple said unless he made a treaty with us, we would lose our reservation, and after only five days of counciling, he urged us to sign the agreement saying, "Unless you sign it, the commissioner will depart tomorrow, etc." And in this manner, undo persuasion was used to get many to sign the so-called agreement who bitterly regret it today.
>
> Out of the Mississippi bands who number about three thousand persons, and who own this reservation in common, less than one hundred persons signed it! Without the consent of a majority of the Mississippi bands, we were made to distinctly understand that the agreement would be null and void, and also, that it would not be binding if the Red Lakers did not consent to consolidate with us.
>
> What we desire is to secure a mutual agreement between the Great Father and ourselves. The White Earth, White Oak Point, and Mille Lacs reservations are owned in common by us, who are called the Mississippi Indians, and if a majority of these Indians consent to an agreement, there will be no trouble between us....The Great Father at Washington should send for the chiefs and leading men of the tribe and talk the matter over with them.

Source: *The Progress* (White Earth Agency, Minnesota), February 4, 1888.

WHITE CLOUD

"My friends, is it the truth?"

HE WHO IS SPOKEN TO and LEADING FEATHER July 6, 1889

IN 1889 yet another commission was sent to the Ojibway of Minnesota, among them the old trader, Henry ("White") Rice, who had long been influential in Ojibway-white dealings. They brought a treaty by which all of the Ojibway reserves in the state would be ceded to the government, except for White Earth and Red Lake; all of the Indians would be removed to these reserves, except for those who chose to take up individual land allotments where they lived. The ceded lands were to be sold for their current value to the highest bidders; the tribe would then receive five percent interest annually on this money for fifty years, and be advanced the sum of $90,000. He Who is Spoken To, the old Red Lake chief, responded to the commissioners on July 6, 1889, with Paul Beaulieu interpreting. He assumed that since white men had brought the Christian faith to him, the commissioners were certain to act and speak with a Christian morality:

> My friends, when you addressed us the first time my eyes were very large, my ears were open[ed] very widely; I understood every thing that you said from the time that you began. I made up my mind that you were men of no common character. I made up my mind that you were men who know how to pity the poor, and to be considerate in dealings.
>
> I, myself, who have been raised a pagan, and don't know anything about religion, am still a believer. I am afraid of Almighty God when I do anything. I am afraid I shall do wrong; I live in constant fear of Him. You certainly will not tell anything but the facts, because we are under the guidance of one Spirit, and certainly the lawmakers who are near our Great Father himself, certainly cannot make up their minds to misrepresent things to us.... I accept your propositions.

The chief's brother, Leading Feather, could not speak with the same assurance:

> My friends, is it the truth?--we don't dispute it, but is it the truth, all that you have said to us--will it transpire? ....The white man is very strong; the Indian is very weak. The white man is high, while the Indian is very low. When an agreement is made the white man always knows how to construe it, but the Indian can not help himself....If the truth is promulgated these people will thank you very much....

Source: Chippewa Indians in Minnesota, in 51 Congress, 1 Session, *House Executive Document*, no. 247, 1889-90 (serial 2747), 81, 83. Leading Feather's name in Ojibway is Nagonegwonabe, not to be confused with Feather's End (Naguanabe) of Mille Lacs, or Sits Ahead (Naganub) of Fond du Lac.

"Instead of looking upon the Indian as a thing, they [the whites] will regard him as an immortal being...."

WHITE CLOUD July 29, 1889

AT WHITE EARTH the new commission dealt with the prominent chief and orator, White Cloud. He brought up many old problems that the Ojibways had with the government, including the dams which had been built which had ruined their rice fields and other aspects of their environment. The commissioners promised to try and have these matters resolved after the new treaty was made. White Cloud, therefore, endorsed the agreement to his people:

> Never was there a negotiation concluded with the Chippewas in which a permanent home was provided for them; this is the first time we have seen it....I am on the brink of the grave, and I leave this as a legacy to you. It is, as it were, my last will and testament. Take this advice as a friend.
>
> Young men, study charity in all its bearings....Do not try to overreach, but be kind to one another, and if you follow these precepts you will have peace and prosperity.... In your intercourse with the whites...politeness and respect on your part will be returned. Instead of looking upon the Indian as a thing, they [the whites] will regard him as an immortal being; they will embrace you in friendship, and consider you as men....

Then, addressing the commissioners, particularly Henry Rice, the chief said:

> See the number of old faces here. We are all growing old; old age brings death; we are all approaching it, and must make the best use of the time before us. I am thinking of the day--and it is sure to come--when you young men, after we are laid away in the grave marked by a mound of earth, when they will say: "This man here spoke in the presence of the truest friend we ever had," and I shall regard it as the proudest monument that shall mark my resting place.

Commissioner Joseph B. Whiting spoke of the chief's advice to his people: "No father could advise his children better; no statesman could advise his people more wisely; so I say that this grand old chief is both father and statesman. See to it then that his words are not lost upon you." White Cloud died nine years later, in 1898, and was succeeded by his son, Charles Wright, an Episcopal minister.

Sources: Chippewa Indians in Minnesota (1889-90), 113-15; *Little Falls Herald*, October 14, 1898.

SHAKES THE RATTLES
IN THE DANCE

"You see that I am now nothing but a corpse...."

SHAKES THE RATTLES IN THE DANCE August 5, 1889

SHAKES THE RATTLES IN THE DANCE (or Shaynowishkung) was born near Inger, Minnesota, in about 1834. He eventually became the leader of a band of Cass Lake Ojibway, later settling near Lake Bemidji. He spoke to commissioners Whiting and Rice on August 5, 1889, questioning the prospects of those Ojibways who might move to White Earth by the so-called Nelson Act:

> **I wish you would listen in pity to my words for only a few moments. You see that I am now nothing but a corpse, but I will try to speak my mind to you. Regarding the proviso for our removal, what shall we do when we get there? Are you going to anchor us there without any subsistence? What shall we get there with? There are alot of Indians who know how to pursue the white man's work, but how shall we subsist when you have anchored us there? I have been a farm hand for ten years. I know the minutia of advancing a farm, although I have not the means of advancing a farm myself. How shall we manage to get ahead so that we can become self-supporting? We will be very much obliged to you if you will please state to us what we may expect when we get there, and what our progress will be.**

The commissioners, per usual, said that they could not promise anything until the bill was passed by Congress. The Nelson Act reached the President and was signed on March 4, 1890. Most of the Ojibways decided against removal probably for the reasons which Shakes the Rattles in the Dance (or "Chief Bemidji") outlined. By September 1893 only 643 people had relocated out of about 4,000. Thus, the attempt to consolidate all of the Ojibways of Minnesota on one or two great reserves had more or less failed. Furthermore, the government policy of giving land allotments to individual Indians eventually resulted in much reservation land passing out of Indian hands and into the possession of the state and federal governments, and various corporations and private land holders. At White Earth, by 1920, only fifteen percent of the reservation was held by the Ojibways; presently only six percent of the reserve is under tribal control.

Sources: Chippewa Indians in Minnesota (1889-90), 116-17; Folwell, *History of Minnesota*, 4:234-35.

APPENDIX ONE: OJIBWAY ORATORS

Bad Boy (Kwiwisensish)--Gull Lake, Mn.
Biajig--Pokegama, Mn.
Broken Tooth (Katawabeda; Fr. Breches dents)--Sandy Lake, Mn.
Buffalo (Pezheke, Beshekee)--Leech Lake, Mn. (see Great Buffalo)
Chingouabe--La Pointe, Madeline Island, Wis.
Crossing Sky (Mayzhuckegeshig)--Rabbit Lake, Mn.
Curly Head (Babesegundiba)--Sandy Lake, Mn.
Feather's End (Naguanabe)--Mille Lacs, Mn.
Flat Mouth I (Eshkebogecoshe; Fr. Gueule Platte)--Leech Lake, Mn.
Flat Mouth II (or Leading Bird of Prey--Negonapinayse, Niganibines)--Leech Lake, Mn.
Foremost Sitter (see Sits Ahead)
Great Buffalo (Kechewaishkee)--La Pointe, Madeline Island, Wis.
Green Setting Feather (Wayshawwushkoquenabe)--Turtle Mountain, No. Dakota and Manitoba
He Who is Spoken To (Maydwaygononind)--Red Lake, Mn.
Hole-in-the-Day I (Pugonageshig, Bugonageshig)--Crow Wing, Mn.
Hole-in-the-Day II (or Boy--Kwiwisens)--Gull Lake, Mn.
Hole-in-the-Sky--Bad River, Wis.
Keeshkemun (Sharpened Stone)--Lac du Flambeau, Wis.
Leading Feather (Nagonegwonabe)--Red Lake, Mn.
Le Couer d'Ours--Lac Court Oreilles, Wis.
Little Boy (Kwiwisens)--Red Lake, Mn.
Little Rock (Aseenewub)--Red Lake, Mn.
Little Six (Shagobe)--Snake River, Mn.
Little Thunder--Red Lake, Mn.
Loon's Foot (Mongozid)--Fond du Lac, Mn.
Majigabo (Great Speaker; Fr. La Trappe)--Leech Lake, Mn.
Manitowab (Sees like God)--Gull Lake, Mn.
Minnehwehna-- Michilimackinac, Michigan
Moose Dung (Monsomo)--Red Lake, Mn.
Moosemani (Moose)--Mille Lacs, Mn.
Nebuneshkung--Gull Lake, Mn.
Red Bear (Miscomukquah)--Pembina, No. Dakota
Shabashkung (He that Passes Under Everything)--Mille Lacs, Mn.
Shakes the Rattles in the Dance (Shaynowwishkung; "Chief Bemidji")--Cass Lake, Mn.
Shingabaossin (Stone Image)--Sault Ste. Marie, Michigan and Ontario
Shokehgeshig--Lake Winnibigoshish, Mn.
Single Man (Lone Man--Piajick)--St. Croix River, Mn. and Wis.
Sits Ahead (Foremost Sitter--Naganub)--Fond du Lac, Mn.
Son of Bear's Heart (Macouda)--Gull Lake, Mn.
Strong Ground (Firm Earth--Songacumig)--Crow Wing, Mn.
Sweet (Weescoup; Fr. Le Sucre)--Red Lake, Mn.
Wadena--Gull Lake, White Fish Lake, Mn.
Warren, William W. --Crow Wing, Mn.
White Cloud (Wabanoquot)--Gull Lake and White Earth, Mn.
White Fisher (Waubojeeg)--Gull Lake, Mn.
White Fisher (Waubojeeg)--LaPointe, Madeline Island, Wis.

APPENDIX TWO: INTERPRETERS of OJIBWAY SPEECHES

Armstrong, Benjamin., 1852 and 1863 trips to Washington
Ashman, Edward., 1855 trip to Washington
Ayer, Frederick., missionary, from 1830s
Ballangier, Joseph, mixed-blood, 1883
Beaulieu, Clement H., mixed-blood trader
Beaulieu, Paul H., mixed-blood, 1863 and 1864 trips to Washington, for agent Edwin Clark, 1866, for the Northwest Commission, 1886
Bonga, Stephen., 1837 treaty negotiations
Boutwell, William., missionary, from 1830s
Brunet, Francis., mixed-blood trader, from 1830s
Cadott, Jean Baptiste., 1783
Cadotte, Jr., Michael, trader
Campbell, Scott., mixed-blood, interpreter for agent Lawrence Taliaferro, 1820-39
Charlo, Charles., from 1830s
Dubay, Jean B., 1837 treaty negotiations
English, M. C., 1889 treaty negotiations
Johnson, John (Enmegahbowh), missionary, from 1840s
Johnston, John., trader
Le Sueur, Pierre Charles., trader, 1695
Madison, Samuel., missionary, 1877 at Red Lake
Marksman, Peter., 1847 treaty negotiations
Montrelle (Montre), Joseph., mixed-blood, trader, from 1830s
Morrison, James G., 1863 and 1864 Washington trips
Perrault, Jean B., trader, 1788
Quinn, Peter., trader, 1837 treaty negotiations
Robert, Joseph., 1881 for Mille Lacs Ojibway
Roy, Peter., principal interpreter for Mississippi Ojibways from 1850s, on 1862, 1863 and 1864 trips to Washington
Warren, Truman A., principal interpreter for Mississippi Ojibways from 1850s
Warren, William W., principal interpreter for Mississippi Ojibways, 1840s--early 1850s
Warren, William V., 1889 negotiations

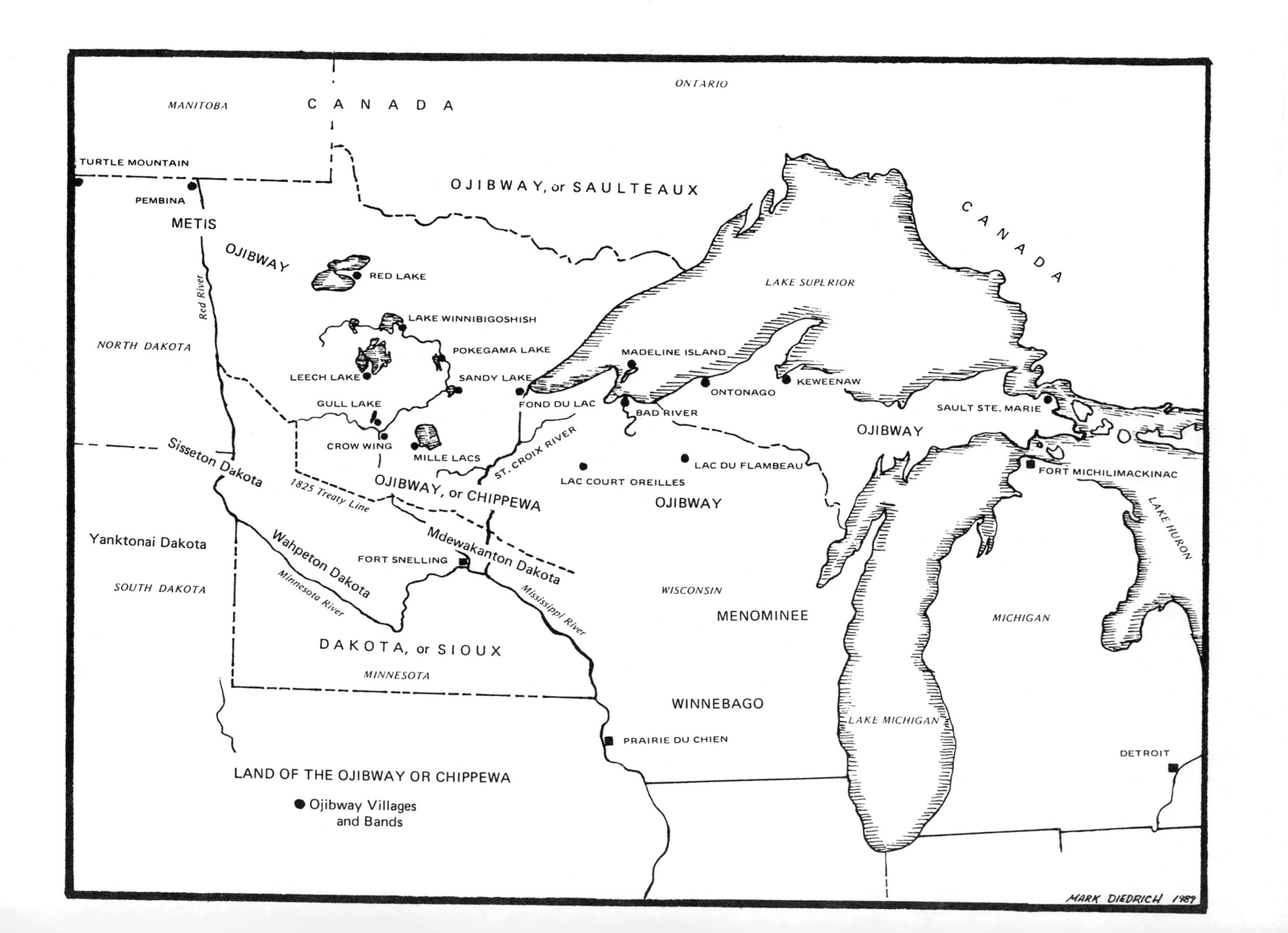

MANITOBA
CANADA
ONTARIO
TURTLE MOUNTAIN
PEMBINA
METIS
OJIBWAY, or SAULTEAUX
CANADA
OJIBWAY
RED LAKE
LAKE SUPLRIOR
Red River
LAKE WINNIBIGOSHISH
NORTH DAKOTA
POKEGAMA LAKE
MADELINE ISLAND
LEECH LAKE
SANDY LAKE
ONTONAGO
KEWEENAW
GULL LAKE
FOND DU LAC
BAD RIVER
SAULT STE. MARIE
OJIBWAY
CROW WING
MILLE LACS
ST. CROIX RIVER
LAC DU FLAMBEAU
Sisseton Dakota
LAC COURT OREILLES
FORT MICHILIMACKINAC
1825 Treaty Line
OJIBWAY, or CHIPPEWA
OJIBWAY
LAKE HURON
Yanktonai Dakota
Wahpeton Dakota
FORT SNELLING
Mdewakanton Dakota
SOUTH DAKOTA
Minnesota River
Mississippi River
WISCONSIN
MENOMINEE
MICHIGAN
DAKOTA, or SIOUX
MINNESOTA
WINNEBAGO
LAKE MICHIGAN
PRAIRIE DU CHIEN
DETROIT
LAND OF THE OJIBWAY OR CHIPPEWA
● Ojibway Villages and Bands
MARK DIEDRICH 1989

BIBLIOGRAPHY

MANUSCRIPTS

American Board of Commissioners for Foreign Missions (ABCFM) Papers, Minnesota Historical Society (MHS), St. Paul
Bassett, Joel., Papers, MHS
Beaulieu, Clement H., Papers, MHS
Flandrau, Charles E., Papers, MHS
Governors' Records, MHS
McKay Papers, McCord Museum, Montreal
Nute, Grace L., Papers (Manuscripts Relating to Northwest Missions), MHS
Office of Indian Affairs (OIA), microfilm copies in MHS
Chippewa Agency, LR
Minnesota Superintendency, LR
St. Peter's Agency, LR
Special File, 201
Winnebago Agency, LR
Ramsey, Alexander., Papers, MHS
Snelling, Josiah., Journal, MHS
Sutherland, James F., Papers, MHS
Taliaferro, Lawrence., Papers, MHS
Thompson, Clark W., Papers, MHS
Whipple, Henry B., Papers, MHS

NEWSPAPERS

Brainerd Dispatch
Galena Daily Advertiser
Henderson Democrat
Little Falls Daily Transcript
Little Falls Herald
Minneapolis Daily Times
Minneapolis Daily Tribune
Minnesota Chronicle and Register (St. Paul)
Minnesota Democrat (St. Paul)
Minnesota Pioneer (St. Paul)
Minnesota Republican (St. Anthony Falls)
Minnesotian (St. Paul)
Niles' Register (Washington)
Progress (White Earth Agency)
St. Cloud Democrat
St. Cloud Journal
St. Paul Daily Globe
St. Paul Daily Press
St. Paul Dispatch
St. Paul Pioneer
St. Paul Pioneer and Democrat

BOOKS AND ARTICLES

Armstrong, Virginia I. comp. *I Have Spoken: American History Through the Voices of the Indians.* Chicago: Sage Books, 1971.
Bird, Harrison. *War for the West: 1790-1813.* New York: Oxford University Press, 1971.
Bray, Edmund C., and Martha C. Bray, eds. *Joseph N. Nicollet on the Plains and Prairies.* St. Paul: Minnesota Historical Society, 1970.
Bray, Martha C., ed. *The Journals of Joseph N. Nicollet.* St. Paul: Minnesota Historical Society, 1970.
Brunson, Alfred. "Sketch of Hole-in-the-Day," *Wisconsin Historical Collections* 5 (1869)387-399.
Coues, Elliott. ed. *The Expeditions of Zebulon Montgomery Pike.* Minneapolis: Ross and Haines, Inc., 1965.
Diedrich, Mark. "Chief Hole-in-the-Day and the 1862 Chippewa Disturbance: A Reappraisal." *Minnesota History* 50 (Spring 1987):193-203.
________. *The Chiefs Hole-in-the-Day of the Mississippi Chippewa.* Minneapolis: Coyote Books, 1986.
________. *Famous Chiefs of the Eastern Sioux.* Minneapolis: Coyote Books, 1987.
Eastman, Mary. *Dahcotah, or Life and Legends of the Sioux Around Fort Snelling.* New York: Arno Press, 1975.
Folwell, William W. *A History of Minnesota.* 4 vols. St. Paul: Minnesota Historical Society, 1921-30.
Gilfillan, J. A. "Ne-bun-esh-kink, The Ideal Soldier." *The Red Man, the School Paper of Carlisle, Pa.* (Jan. 1913):194-98.
Guthman, William H. *March to Massacre, A History of the First Seven Years of the United States Army, 1784-1791.* New York: McGraw-Hill Book Co., 1970.
Hodge, Frederick W. ed. *Handbook of American Indians.* Part 2. Totowa, NJ: Rowman and Littlefield, 1979.
Kohl, Johann G. *Kitchi-Gami, Life Among the Lake Superior Ojibway.* St. Paul: Minnesota Historical Society Press, 1985.
Levi, M. C. *Chippewa Indians of Yesterday and Today.* New York: Pageant Press, Inc., 1956.
Lewis, Henry. *The Valley of the Mississippi Illustrated.* Bertha L. Heilbron, ed. St. Paul: Minnesota Historical Society, 1967.
McKenney, Thomas L. and James Hall. *The Indian Tribes of North America.* 3 vols. Edinburgh: J. Grant, 1933.
McKenney, Thomas L. *Sketches of a Tour to the Lakes.* Minneapolis: Ross and Haines, Inc., 1959.
Morse, Richard E. "The Chippewas of Lake Superior." *Wisconsin Historical Collections* 3 (1857):338-369.
Neill, Edward D. "History of the Ojibways." in William W. Warren, *History of the Ojibway.* Minneapolis: Ross and Haines, Inc., 1974.
Ojibway Chiefs' Speech to Major May, Sept. 8, 1797, in *Michigan Pioneer and Historical Collections* 8 (1907):506.
Peckham, Howard H. *Pontiac and the Indian Uprising.* Chicago: Phoenix Books, 1961.
Perrault, Jean B. "Narrative of the Travels and Adventures, 1783-1820." *Michigan Pioneer and Historical Collections* 37 (1909-10):508-619.
Proceedings of a Council with the Chippewa Indians. *The Iowa Journal of History and Politics* 9 (1911):408-434.
[Ramsey, Alexander]. *Miscellaneous Pamphlets* Vol. 2, no. 25 (in the Minnesota Historical Society library, St. Paul).
Schoolcraft, Henry R. *Information Respecting the History, Condition, and Prospects of the Indian Tribes of the United States* Part 2. Philadelphia: Lippincott, Grambo and Company, 1852.
________. *The Literary Voyage; or Muzzeniegun.* Philip P. Mason, ed. East Lansing, Michigan: Michigan State University Press, 1962.
________. *Personal Memoirs.* Philadelphia: Lippincott, Grambo and Company, 1851.
________. *Schoolcraft's Expedition to Lake Itasca.* Philip P. Mason, ed. East Lansing: Michigan State University Press, 1958.
United States Congress. House and Senate Executive Documents and Reports. Serial Set: 777, 1157, 2449, 2747.
Warren, William W. *History of the Ojibway.* Minneapolis: Ross and Haines, Inc., 1974.
Weeks, Helen C. [Campbell]. *White and Red; A Narrative of Life Among the Northwest Indians.* New York: Hurd and Houghton Cambridge Press, 1869.
Whipple, Henry B. *Lights and Shadows of a Long Episcopate.* New York: Macmillan Co., 1899.
________. "Civilization and Christianization of the Ojibways in Minnesota." *Minnesota Historical Collections* 9 (1901):
Williams, Mentor L. ed. *Henry R. Schoolcraft, Narrative Journal of Travels.* Lansing: Michigan State College Press, 1953.